A Guide with Models for Process Writing

モデルで学ぶ
プロセス・ライティング入門

SHOHAKUSHA

Written by Miki Shibata

はじめに

本書はプロセス・ライティングというアプローチに基づいて、パラグラフを書く練習をするためのテキストです。相手に自分の意図を理解してもらえる文章を書くためには、文法と語彙だけが重要なのではなく、文章構成と個々の文のつながりが大切です。首尾一貫した文章が書けるようになるため、段階を追って一歩ずつ進めていきます。

このテキストのもうひとつの特徴は、よい文をまねることです。外国語学習の上達、特にリスニング力をつけるためには、その言語にできるだけたくさん触れることがカギだと言われています。インプットの中に初めて耳にする、知らない表現が出てくると「分からない」と思います。そして、その表現がインプットの中に繰り返し出てくると、辞書で調べたり先生に聞いたりします。そして、その表現が理解できるようになると、今度はスピーキングのときに使えるようになります。このプロセスはライティングにも当てはまると思います。つまり、文のインプットにたくさん触れることです。外国語がまだ十分でないうちは、言いたいことを文にすることですら大変です。しかし、文がうまく書けないからと言って、文章が書けないことにはなりません。そこで、このテキストでは、インプットとして例文をたくさん提示しました。自分の伝えたいことを表していると思う文を選んで組み合わせていくことで、文章構成に注意を払い全体が見えるように考えてあります。語彙力をつけるために単語を覚えることと同じで、例文をまねることで文章力の基礎となる「文力」をつけていきましょう。(注)

以上、文章を書くために段階を経ること、例文をまねることを説明しました。ただし、この2つのことが功を成すには、みなさんが次の3つに留意する必要があります。

(1) 忍耐強く

書く作業には時間とエネルギーが必要です。特に、実際に書き始める前はアイデアや考えをまとめる段階に時間がかかります。しかし、この作業は非常に大切なことなので、じっくりと「自分は何を伝えたいのか」を明確にします。時間をかけて「何をどのように書くか」を考えることで、論理的で整合性のある文章になります。

また、一度で分かりやすい文章は書けません。パラグラフを書き終わったらしばらく時間をおいて読み返します。自分で書いた文章であるにもかかわらず、「ここは何を言いたかったのだろう?」と分からない箇所が出てきます。時には説明不足やまわりくどい文に気がつくでしょう。そうした不適切なところを、文の追加や削除、言い換えをすることによってさらに分かりやすい文章にしていきます。

(2) 意識する

文章を書き上げるためには、「内容や構成を考える」、「ドラフトを書く」、「推敲する」、「ドラフトを書き直す」など複数の段階があります。また、「どのような情報が必要か」、「どの語句を使うか」、「どのような文体を用いるか」、「どのように説明をしたらよいか」、「文と文をどのようにつなげるとよいか」など考えなければならないことがたくさんあります。ところが、これら全てを同時に行うことは無理です。分かりやすいパラグラフを書くためには、それぞれの段階で「今は、何をしなければならない段階なのか」、「今、集中すべき作業は何か」を意識し、ひとつずつ積み上げていくことが大切です。

(3) 責任を持つ

最終的な英作文を提出するまでに何度も書き直しをします。書き直しにあたっては、3つの方法があります。おそらく最初に思いつくのは、先生に添削をしてもらうことでしょう。しかし、先生に不適切な箇所をすべて指摘、訂正してくれることを望むのではなく、自分で訂正できるところはまず自分で行うという姿勢で取り組みましょう。従って、自分の文章を自分で読み返し不明瞭な箇所を修正することもひとつの方法です。つまり、先生からの一方的な添削に頼るのではなく、自分の作文力向上に自分で責任を持つことを自覚します。

3つ目の方法として、クラスメートからの意見やコメントも有益です。「英語があまり得意ではないので、コメントなどできない」という学生がいますが、正しいコメントはありません。また、「クラスメートの英作文がよく理解できないのは、私の英語力のせいだ」と嘆く学生もいますが、必ずしも英語力の問題ではありません。つまり、「十分に説明がされていない」、「文のつながりが示されていない」など、書き手に問題があるため理解できないことがあるのです。クラスメートの英作文にコメントをすることは、文法の間違いを指摘することではありません。内容に関して分からないところや思ったことを率直に書いてあげましょう。

書き直しにあたっては、先生やクラスメートからの訂正やコメントを鵜呑みにする必要は全くありません。どれを採用するかはあなた自身で決めてください。先生からのコメントでさえ全てをそのまま受け入れる必要はないのです。やはりここでも自分で考えることが大切です。ライティングに正解はありません。

2014年
柴田美紀

(注) ただし、他人によって書かれた文章を何の断りもなくそのまま写すのは、剽窃(ひょうせつ)です。しかし、このテキストは文章のまねを奨励しているのではなく、あくまでインプットとして例文を提示しています。

Contents

Starter	Prewriting Task 始める前に——自分で書いてみよう	4
Chapter 1	Writing Process & Prewriting Stage ライティング・プロセスと準備段階を理解する	7
Chapter 2	Paragraph Organization パラグラフ構成を理解する	16
Chapter 3	Describe Your Personality 自分の性格を描写してみよう	25
Chapter 4	Revision：Describe Your Personality ドラフトの修正——描写する	33
Chapter 5	Contrasting Two Countries 二つの国を比較してみよう	38
Chapter 6	Revision：Contrasting Two Countries ドラフトの修正——比較する	48
Chapter 7	Analyzing Reasons & Results 理由と結果を分析してみよう	52
Chapter 8	Revision：Analyzing Reasons & Results ドラフトの修正——分析する	66
Chapter 9	Giving Suggestion 解決策を提案してみよう	70
Chapter 10	Revision：Giving Suggestion ドラフトの修正——提案する	84
Chapter 11	Stating Your Opinion 自分の意見を述べてみよう	88
Chapter 12	Revision：Stating Your Opinion ドラフトの修正——意見を述べる	104
Sentence Exercises		108
Appendices		111

Starter

Prewriting Task

外国語学習について書いてください。外国語学習が役に立った経験、あるいは外国語を勉強しておけばよかったと思った経験、外国語学習の必要性、理想的な外国語勉強法など、外国語学習に関することであれば、内容は自由です。

You can use the blank space below freely. ： 以下の余白を自由に使ってください。

Chapter 1
Writing Process & Prewriting Stage

The main points of this chapter are as follows:

◆ What is a process writing approach?

◆ What stages do you go through in order to produce a final written work?

◆ What preparation do you need to do before actually writing?

この章のポイントは以下の通りです。

◆ プロセス・ライティング・アプローチとは何か。

◆ 最終稿を仕上げるまでにどのような段階を経るのか。

◆ 実際に書く前にどのような準備をする必要があるのか。

1-1. A process writing approach　プロセス・ライティング・アプローチ

Writing is communication! We would like to convey a message to readers through writing. It is ideal for them to understand our intention without difficulty. Unlike speaking, however, we cannot explain the main point of a story to them face to face. Given this, it is necessary to provide enough information and details in an appropriate way. This awareness should lead you to good writing.

Then, what do we need to do in order to write a comprehensible paragraph? It is not possible to write it easily from the beginning. Writing is not a single process, but can be divided into multiple processes. Completing each stage leads to a good paragraph. This is **a process writing approach** in such reaching to a final piece of work through steps.

「書く」とは、コミュニケーションです。書くことで読み手にメッセージを伝えようとします。読み手に無理なくメッセージを分かってもらえるのが理想です。ところが、話す場合と異なり、面と向かって趣旨を読み手に直接説明することができません。従って、読み手がこちらの意図を十分理解するだけの情報や詳細を、適切な方法で提供する必要があります。この点を意識することが上手なライティングにつながっていくでしょう。

では、分かりやすい文章を書くために、具体的にどのような作業が必要なのでしょうか。最初から分かりやすい文章はすぐには書けません。ライティングは一回で終わる作業ではなく、実はいくつものプロセスに分けられ、そのひとつひとつを完了することで最終的によい文章につながっていきます。このようにライティングをいくつかの異なる作業に分けて文章をしあげていく方法が**プロセス・ライティング・アプローチ**です。

1-2. Stages in a writing process　複数の段階に分けられるライティング

Writing is a process with a series of four stages that lead to a final draft.

ファイナル・ドラフトを書き上げるまでに、ライティングは4つの段階に分けられます。

1. Prewriting stage［プレ・ライティングの段階］: The first step is generating ideas. You think of a topic and narrow it down from general information to specific information by brainstorming.

   最初の段階では、何を書くかを考えます。その際、ブレイン・ストーミングをして明確で具体的なトピックを考えます。

2. Drafting stage［ドラフトの段階］: You actually write. Focus on the content and plot development without worrying too much about grammar and any mechanical issues such as spelling.

   ここでは、実際に作文をします。ただし、下書きの段階なので、文法やスペルなどはあまり心配せず内容やパラグラフ構成に集中します。

3. Revising stage［修正の段階］: You read your first draft and rethink the content. You can add necessary information or cut unrelated ideas and details and change the order of ideas. You should also review and rewrite individual sentences to be more comprehensible.

   ファースト・ドラフトを読み直し、内容を再考する段階です。必要な情報やことがらを追加したり、トピックに関係のない不必要なものを削ったりします。あるいは、情報やことがらなどの順番を変えてみるのもよいでしょう。また、各文を吟味し書き直すことでより分かりやすい文章になっていきます。

4. Editing stage［編集の段階］: You work on grammar and mechanical aspects of your written work. Double-check spelling, capitalization, and grammar. Your ideas and details should be finalized with little modification at this stage.

   この段階では、細かいところを修正します。スペル、大文字、文法などです。ただし、アイデアを変更するなど内容に関わる大がかりな修正は行いません。

The stages described above do not always progress sequentially. As shown below, you go back and forth among the stages.

「書く」プロセスは、上で説明した段階が直線的に進むのではなく、以下に示すようにこれらの段階を行ったり来たりします。

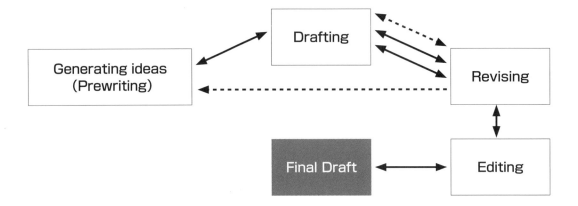

In particular, you go back and forth between drafting and revising stages many times. As you can see in the figure, you cannot write a good paragraph immediately. You need to go through these stages repeatedly until completing your final draft.

特にドラフトと修正の段階は何度も行ったり来たりします。この図から分かるように、よい文章はすぐには書けないのです。これらの段階を行ったり来たりしながら、最終的によい文章が出来上がっていきます。

When you revise your draft ...
Revise your draft to make it more clear and comprehensible. Three major ways help you think about what parts to revise and how you should revise your draft. First of all, you should read what you have written and check whether the passage conveys your main point appropriately. Next, it is also useful to receive feedback or comments from your teacher. Finally, ask your classmates for comments as well. They should be as useful as your teacher's advice.

修正をするときに…
より明確で分かりやすい文章にするためにドラフトを修正します。どこをどのように修正すればよいかを考えるために3つの方法があります。まず、書き終わったものを自分で読み返してみて、文章がメイン・ポイントを適切に伝えているかを確認します。次に、先生からフィードバックとしてコメントをもらうことも有益です。そして、3つ目にクラスメートにドラフトを読んでもらいコメントをもらう方法があります。先生からのアドバイスと同じように、クラスメートからのコメントも役に立ちます。

1-3. Prewriting Stage　プレ・ライティングの段階

Good writers do not start writing right away. They go through some processes before actually writing. What processes are involved in the prewriting stage?

書くことが上手な人は、いきなり書き始めません。実際に書き始める前に準備をします。では、プレ・ライティングの段階では、具体的にどのようなことをするのでしょうか。

Step 1　Brainstorming　ブレイン・ストーミング

Generate ideas to work with in your writing. Let your ideas come out freely; whatever ideas you can think of, write them down. Do not worry whether the ideas are good or not and whether they fit the topic well. Don't worry about writing complete or grammatical sentences or putting anything in order.

パラグラフを書くためのアイデアを出していきます。頭に浮かんだことをどんどん書いていきましょう。「アイデアが適切かどうか」、「トピックにふさわしいかどうか」などは一切気にせず、ひたすら書き出してみましょう。ブレイン・ストーミングをしているときは、アイデアを文で書き表したり文法を気にしたり、またアイデアの順番も気にする必要はありません。

How to brainstorm

There are different ways to brainstorm, as suggested below.

以下にあるように、ブレイン・ストーミングには異なった方法があります。

a. Clustering

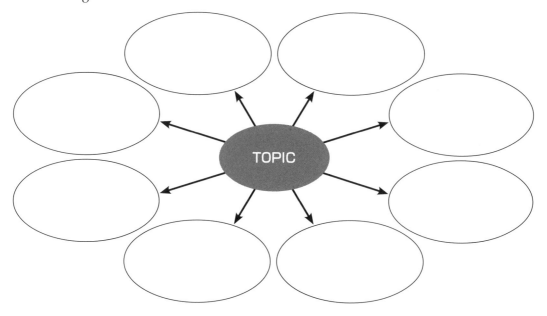

b. Listing

1. _____
2. _____
3. _____
4. _____
5. _____

c. Discussion : You will discuss the topic in a group. Tell your thoughts and listen to others, which should help you find new ideas and perspectives about the topic.

トピックについてグループで話し合いをします。自分の意見を聞いてもらったり、他の人の考えを聞いたりします。そうすることで、トピックに関して新しいアイデアや見方が発見できるでしょう。

Exercise 1.1

Go back to your first writing and brainstorm for ideas on the topic. Cluster or list your thoughts and ideas about *foreign language learning*.

最初のライティング・タスクに戻って、トピックについてブレイン・ストーミングをしてみましょう。「外国語学習」について考えやアイデアを書き出してみましょう。

Step 2 Narrowing down a topic トピックをしぼる

You should have come up with many ideas for a theme in the brainstorming stage. Now, you want to narrow them down and choose a clear and concrete topic. There are a lot of topics you could write about *foreign language learning*. For example,

ブレイン・ストーミングではひとつのトピックについていろいろなアイデアを出しました。次は、アイデアをしぼって、明確で具体的なトピックへとつなげます。「外国語学習」というトピックについてもたくさんのことが書けます。
例えば、関連するアイデアとして、

◆ Advantages of learning a foreign language

◆ My way of studying a foreign language

◆ Learning culture through foreign language learning

◆ The pleasure of foreign language learning

◆ 外国語学習の利点

◆ 私の外国語学習法

◆ 外国語学習を通して学ぶ文化

◆ 外国語学習の楽しさ

Exercise 1.2

What would you like to write about on the topic of *foreign language learning*? Narrow down your ideas to a more specific topic.

「外国語学習」についてどのようなことを書こうと思いますか。より具体的なトピックになるようにしぼってみましょう。

Step 3 Developing a main idea for the topic　トピックのメイン・アイデアを考える

Once you have decided on the specific topic, you need to create a main idea. You have to think about what point you would like to emphasize in your writing.

十分検討してトピックが明確で具体的なものになったら、メイン・アイデアを考えます。つまり、そのトピックについてこれから書く文章で何を強調し、読者に何を伝えたいのかを考えます。

For example, when your topic is about the advantages of learning a foreign language, you need to decide on what advantages you are going to focus in your writing. Some possible main ideas appear as follows :

例えば、外国語学習の利点をトピックに決めたら、どのような利点に焦点を当てるかを考えます。考えられる利点としては、次のようなものがあげられます。

a. *The knowledge of the German language and culture that I had learned at the university helped me when I was on a trip to Europe.*

a. ヨーロッパ旅行のとき、大学で学習したドイツ語とドイツ文化の知識が役に立った。

b. *We can become aware of the values of our own culture when we study a foreign language.*

b. 外国語を勉強すると、自分の文化に対して価値を見い出すことができる。

c. *When we study a foreign language, we realize that we interpret the world differently depending on our language background.*

c. 外国語を勉強すると、言語によって世界の見方が異なると気づく。

The main idea should focus on only one thought. Look at the example below :

メイン・アイデアはひとつのポイントに焦点を当てます。次の例を見てみましょう。

Example of a poor main idea

Learning a foreign language will give us a chance to realize how great our own culture is and how difficult it is to learn grammar.

The example shows two ideas : *realizing how great our own culture is and realizing how difficult it is to learn grammar*. The writer should decide which one she or he would like to discuss in the paragraph.

不適切なメイン・アイデアの例

外国語学習を通して、自らの文化のすばらしさに気づき、また文法学習の難しさを実感する。

この例は、2つのアイデアが含まれています。ひとつ目は「自らの文化のすばらしさに気づく」、もうひとつは「文法学習の難しさを実感する」です。これらの2つはそれぞれが異なる内容になりますので、どちらか一方をメイン・アイデアとして選びます。

Exercise 1.3

Think about what you would like to focus on for the topic you narrowed down in Exercise 1.2. Then, write your main idea.

Exercise 1.2でしぼったトピックについて、どのような内容にするかを考えてみましょう。そして、メイン・アイデアを具体的に書いてみましょう。

_____

_____

_____

_____

Group Work 1

Compare your main ideas in groups of three.

3人でグループを作って、お互いのメイン・アイデアを比べてみましょう。

Chapter 2
Paragraph Organization

The main points of this chapter are as follows:

◆ How should a paragraph be organized?

◆ What is a topic sentence?

◆ What is a concluding sentence?

◆ What is a good title?

この章のポイントは以下の通りです。

◆ パラグラフをどのように構成するべきか。

◆ 話題文 (topic sentence) とは何か。

◆ 結論文 (concluding sentence) とは何か。

◆ よいタイトルとはどのようなタイトルか。

2-1. Structure of a paragraph　パラグラフ構成

The basic structure of a paragraph consists of three major parts : a topic sentence, a body, and a concluding sentence. The body is further made up of main points and supporting sentences. Main points are necessary in order to explain the main idea described in the topic sentence; supporting sentences should explain each main point. The paragraph organization should look as follows :

パラグラフは基本的に話題文、本文、結論文の3つから構成されています。本文はさらに複数のメイン・ポイントと複数の支持文から成り立っています。メイン・ポイントは、話題文で述べている主張（メイン・アイデア）を裏づけるために必要です。そして支持文は各メイン・ポイントを具体的に説明します。パラグラフの構成は以下のようになります。

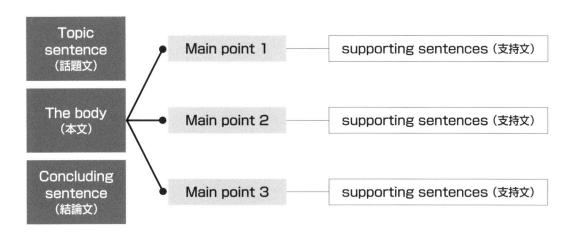

2-2. Writing a topic sentence　話題文を書く

A paragraph starts with a topic sentence. The topic sentence plays a very important role since it indicates the main idea of a whole paragraph. In other words, the reader can find out what the paragraph is about through reading the topic sentence.

パラグラフは話題文で始めます。話題文はパラグラフ全体のメイン・アイデアを示しているので、とても重要な役割を果たしています。つまり、読者は話題文を読むことで、パラグラフが何について書かれているかを知ることができるのです。

In order to write an effective topic sentence, follow these suggestions :

効果的な話題文を書くためには以下のことに注意します。

● An affirmative sentence is best for a topic sentence. Of course, questions and exclamatory sentences can appear in the essay; however, the topic sentence is always an affirmative sentence in this textbook since our focus is on academic writing.

話題文は肯定文が望ましいでしょう。もちろん、エッセイなどでは話題文が疑問文や感嘆文で書かれていることもありますが、このテキストではアカデミック・ライティングに焦点を当てているので、肯定文とします。

● The topic sentence should convey one main idea. For this reason, the topic needs to be narrowed down to be specific enough at the pre-writing stage.

話題文はひとつのメイン・アイデアだけを表します。そのためには、プレ・ライティングの段階でトピックを十分に具体的なものにしておく必要があります。

Exercise 2.1

Write a topic sentence for the topic of *foreign language learning*.

外国語学習のトピックに話題文を書いてみましょう。

Your topic sentence : _____

Group Work 2.1

Compare your topic sentences in groups of three. Give some comments on each member's topic sentence.

3人でグループを作って、お互いの話題文を比べます。そして、お互いコメントをしてみましょう。

2-3. Writing the body　本文を書く

Once you have written a topic sentence, you need to think about how to support the main idea addressed in the topic sentence.

話題文を書いたら、次は話題文で主張していること（メイン・アイデア）をどのように支持するかを考えます。

The body section, which is the longest part of the paragraph, consists of sentences that support the main idea : the main points plus supporting sentences that explain each of the main

本文はメイン・アイデアを支持する複数の文（メイン・ポイントとそれらを説明する支持文）からなっていて、パラグラフの中で一番長い部分です。重要なことは、話題文のポイントに関係する文だけを、お互いの文のつながり（順序）も

points. Importantly, this section includes only sentences related to the topic, and they should be connected to each other.

考えて書くことです。

Point 1　Coherence and cohesion　一貫性と結束性

A paragraph is considered good when individual sentences relate to only one main idea (*coherence*) and are logically connected to each other (*cohesion*). Even when the sentences discuss only one main idea, the paragraph is not well organized unless the sentences are carefully presented in a logical order. In order to avoid confusion for readers, it is necessary to think about what order of sentences makes the paragraph flow.

全ての文がひとつのメイン・アイデアに関わり（一貫性：coherence）、個々の文がお互い論理的に関係している（結束性：cohesion）とき、よいパラグラフと見なされます。全ての文が同じトピックのことについて書かれていることはもちろんですが、文の順序が不適切で前後の文がつながっていなければ、パラグラフはまとまりを持ちません。読者の混乱を避けるためには、どのような順序で文を書くとパラグラフが流れるのかを考える必要があります。

Point 2　Linking signals　つなぎのサイン

Linking signals play an important role in coherence. Depending on the writing genre (i.e., narration, description, comparison/contrast, or exposition), the sentences are connected with different linking signals.

文と文をつなぐ方法のひとつとして連結語句があります。書くジャンル（物語、記述、比較対照、説明など）によって連結語句は異なります。

Step 1　Outlining the main points　メイン・ポイントのアウトラインを考える

Choose some ideas from the group of ideas that you have generated through brainstorming to support your main idea. You can also add new ideas. These are your main points. Then, put them in order to make your argument comprehensible to readers. That is, outlining should help you logically order your main points and lead to the conclusion without difficulty.

話題文で書いた主張を支持するために必要なことがらを複数選択します。ブレイン・ストーミングで出したいくつかのアイデアの中から、あるいは新たに関係する項目を追加して、支持に必要なポイント（メイン・ポイント）を選びます。そして、読者に主張を理解してもらえるようにこれらのポイントを順番に並べます。このようにアウトラインを考えることは、メイン・ポイントを論理的な順番で並べ、無理なく結論へとつなげていくために有益な作業です。

Step 2 — Writing supporting sentences to explain the main points　メイン・ポイントを説明する支持文を書く

After outlining your main points, you need to explain each of them with supporting sentences. They should provide enough information and evidence so that the reader can follow your argument.

メイン・ポイントのアウトラインができたら、それぞれのメイン・ポイントを支持文で説明します。支持文は情報や証拠となることがらを過不足なく示すことで、読者が議論に無理なくついてこられるようにします。

2-4. Writing a concluding sentence　結論文を書く

Write a concluding sentence at the end of the paragraph. Like the topic sentence, the concluding sentence indicates the most important point (main idea) in the paragraph.

パラグラフの最後は、結論文です。話題文のようにパラグラフの最も重要なポイント（メイン・アイデア）を書きます。

● The concluding sentence summarizes the content of the paragraph. This reminds the reader of the main idea in the paragraph.

結論文でパラグラフの内容を要約します。そうすることで読者が再度パラグラフのメイン・アイデアを思い起こすことができます。

● The concluding sentence should be consistent with the topic sentence. Rephrase the topic sentence for the concluding sentence.

結論文は話題文と首尾一貫した内容でなければなりません。話題文を言い換えて、結論文とします。

● Do not introduce any new ideas in the concluding sentence. If you bring up new information, readers will be confused since they expect you to finish the paragraph.

結論文では新しいことは導入しません。新しいことを述べると、パラグラフが終了すると思っていた読者が混乱してしまいます。

Exercise 2.2

Read the following paragraphs. Write a concluding sentence for each one.

次のパラグラフを読んで、結論文を書いてみましょう。

1

   The experience of learning a new language makes us realize the uniqueness of different cultures. We tend to expect people from different cultures to behave and think the same way as we do; on the contrary, people with different language backgrounds do the same things in different ways. For example, indirectness is the most appropriate communication strategy for Japanese. In other words, they are expected to address others using an indirect way of speaking. However, this does not necessarily work with non-Japanese. They prefer direct speech since they express their thoughts directly.

2

   Individual differences can predict success or failure in language learning. Students' personality, their intellectual ability, their motivation, and their age can be associated with success in learning a foreign language. Depending on these differences, some students progress rapidly while others struggle, making very slow progress. For example, many teachers believe that outgoing learners who interact without hesitation in a foreign language and seek opportunities to practice language skills will be the most successful learners. Also, the younger the students are, the more successfully they seem to achieve native-like proficiency.

Respond to the following questions to review your concluding sentences. You may want to rewrite it if either of your responses is NO.

次の質問に答えて結論文をチェックしてみましょう。回答に「いいえ」があれば、結論文を書き直してみましょう。

1	Does your concluding sentence summarize the main point by rephrasing the topic sentence? 話題文を言い換えた表現でメイン・アイデアが要約されていますか。	はい・いいえ
2	Did you avoid introducing any new information or ideas in your concluding sentence? 結論文に新しい情報やアイデアが書かれていませんか。	はい・いいえ

Group Work 2.2

Make groups of three. Share the concluding sentences that you have written for Exercise 2.2 with your group members.

3人でグループを作って、Exercise 2.2で書いた結論文を比べてみましょう。

2-5. Writing a Title　タイトルを書く

A title represents the topic of your paragraph : it gives readers an idea of what the paragraph is about. Moreover, an attractive title motivates people to read your passage.

タイトルはパラグラフのトピックを表します。従って、読者はタイトルから、パラグラフが何について書かれているかを考えることができます。また、読者がタイトルに興味を持てば、パラグラフを読んでみようという気持ちになります。

A title should have the features described below :

タイトルは、次のような特徴があります。

- The title should be a noun phrase, not a sentence, in academic writing. Examples 1 and 2 below should be avoided since they are an affirmative sentence and a question, respectively. Since this book focuses on academic writing, you are encouraged to write titles as noun phrases. Given this, both examples should be rewritten into The Importance of Friends.

    Example 1 : Friends Are Important ⇒ The Importance of Friends
    Example 2 : Why Are Friends Important? ⇒ The Importance of Friends

    アカデミックなライティングでのタイトルは、名詞句が一般的です。その意味で、文で書かれたExample 1や疑問文のExample 2は避けるべきです。このテキストはアカデミック・ライティングを中心としているので、タイトルは名詞句で書くことを奨励します。Example 1とExample 2はいずれもThe Importance of Friendsに書き換えるのが望ましいでしょう。

- The title should be specific enough to give the reader some idea about the paragraph. Example 1 below is too general. On the other hand, Example 2 should be specific enough for the reader to know what the paragraph is about. From the title, we can guess that the writer and his/her family treat their dog like a family member and that he or she will write about it.

    Example 1 : Pets
    Example 2 : Dogs as Family Members

読者にパラグラフの内容が想像できるように具体的なタイトルにします。ひとつ目の例は、一般的で大まかすぎます。一方、2つ目のタイトルは具体的で、書き手とその家族が家族の一員として犬と接していることがパラグラフに書かれているだろうと予測できます。

Exercise 2.3

Choose the one that would make the most appropriate title.

タイトルとして最も適切だと思うものをひとつ選んでみましょう。

(1) a. I Like My Sister
　　b. The Reason Why Siblings Are Important
　　c. The Value of Siblings

(2) a. Difficulty of Changing People's Minds
　　b. What I Learned from Waiting Patiently
　　c. My Mistake

(3) a. Health
　　b. Diet is the Savior for Fat People
　　c. The Necessity of Moderate Exercise

Group Work 2.3

Share your answers for Exercise 2.3 in groups of three. Make sure you explain the reasons for your choices.

3人でグループを作って、Exercise 2.3で選んだタイトルについて話してみましょう。最も適切だと思った理由も説明してください。

Chapter 3
Describe Your Personality

Chapter 3 focuses on personality. You will describe your personality with adjectives.

第3章では性格を取りあげます。自身の性格を形容詞で描写してみましょう。

Step 1 Brainstorming to generate ideas

Do the following adjectives describe your personality?　　次の形容詞はあなたの性格に当てはまりますか？

	English	日本語	Are you …?
1	active		YES ・ NO
2	ambitious		YES ・ NO
3	competitive		YES ・ NO
4	considerate		YES ・ NO
5	creative		YES ・ NO
6	dependable		YES ・ NO
7	honest		YES ・ NO
8	modest		YES ・ NO
9	opinionated		YES ・ NO
10	patient		YES ・ NO
11	positive		YES ・ NO
12	responsible		YES ・ NO
13	shy		YES ・ NO
14	sociable		YES ・ NO
15	talkative		YES ・ NO

Expression bank

Expressions	Examples
to participate in	I like to participate in social events on campus.
to join	I joined a community volunteer group.
to be eager to ~	I am eager to help elderly people in the community.
to be involved in	I am involved in the campus newspaper committee.
to take lessons	I am now taking flower arrangement lessons once a week.
face-to-face conversation	I am not good at talking to people in face-to-face conversations.
to be reluctant to ~	I am reluctant to speak up in class.
to hesitate to ~	I hesitate to express my opinion openly to others.
to trust	My friends trust me because I am dependable.
to rely on	I rely on my family financially.
to lie/tell a lie	I consider myself honest and do not like to lie to others.
to achieve/accomplish	I try hard to achieve my goals.
to pursue	I would like to pursue my academic interest in graduate school.
to state/give/express one's opinion (on ~)	I hesitate to state/give/express my opinions on politics.

Considering your own behavior, choose three adjectives that describe you most appropriately.

自分の行動パターンを観察して、自身の性格を最も適切に描写していると思う形容詞を3つ選んでみましょう。

Adjective (1) _____

Adjective (2) _____

Adjective (3) _____

Step 2 Writing a topic sentence

Write a topic sentence (TS) that includes the three adjectives you have chosen above. Refer to the examples below :

上で選んだ3つの形容詞を使って話題文を書いてみましょう。以下の例を参考にしてください。

> [TS1] In terms of characteristics, I am generally active, talkative, and opinionated.
> [TS2] The following adjectives best describe my personality : modest, shy, and responsible.
> [TS3] I can be described with three adjectives : dependable, considerate, and talkative.
> [TS4] The following three adjectives adequately describe my character : ambitious, competitive, and patient.
> [TS5] Three adjectives—creative, sociable, and honest—adequately describe my personality.

Write your topic sentence.

_____

Step 3 Writing the body

▶ 【Sub-step 1】 Outlining the main points

Write main points that describe your characteristics after consulting the examples below :

以下の例を参考にして、自身の性格を描写するメイン・ポイントを書いてみましょう。

> Main point (MP) 1 : I am a shy person. / I am shy.
> Main point (MP) 2 : I am an active person. / I am active.
> Main point (MP) 3 : I am a creative person. / I am creative.

MP1 _____

MP2 _____

MP3 _____

▶ 【Sub-step 2】 Writing supporting sentences

Write supporting sentences for your main points above. Refer to the sentence patterns in the examples below.

メイン・ポイントを説明する支持文を書いてみましょう。文体は以下の例を参考にしてください。

Examples

MP1 : I am a shy person. / I am shy.

> I am reluctant to raise my hand in class to present my opinion.
>
> I introduce myself only when someone asks me my name.

supporting sentences for main point 1

MP2 : I am an active person. / I am active.

> I am involved in many school activities.
>
> I take yoga lessons three times a week.

supporting sentences for main point 2

MP3 : I am a creative person. / I am creative.

> I like sewing and knitting and make my own clothes.
>
> I take a sketchbook with me on trips because I love drawing landscapes.

supporting sentences for main point 3

 **Remember !**

Coherence and cohesion should be the focus at this stage, so you might not want to pay too much attention to grammatical accuracy.

ここでは、文章の一貫性と結束性を考えることが大切ですので、文法の正確さにそれほど注意を向ける必要はありません。

Write your supporting sentences for each of your main points.

(1) _____

_____

_____

(2) _____

_____

_____

(3) _____

_____

_____

Step 4 Writing a concluding sentence

Write a concluding sentence (CS). The CS must be the rephrased TS starting with a linking phrase. See the linking phrase box and example sentences below for reference.

結論文を書いてみましょう。結論文はつなぎの語句から始まり、話題文を言い換えた文です。以下のつなぎの語句と例を参考にしてください。

Linking Phrase Box

> To sum up,
> In conclusion,

[CS1] I am an active, talkative, and opinionated person.
[CS2] I can be described with the three adjectives modest, shy, and responsible.
[CS3] I can best be described as dependable, considerate, and talkative.
[CS4] I am ambitious, competitive, and patient.
[CS5] The three adjectives creative, sociable, and honest adequately describe me.

Step 5 Writing a title

Write a title for your paragraph. It should help readers predict what the main point is in the paragraph. See the examples below.

タイトルをつけてみましょう。読む人が文章の内容を想像できるタイトルを考えます。以下の例を参考にしてください。

> ① My Personality
> ② Personality Type
> ③ Three Adjectives That Describe Me
> ④ The Type of Person I Am

Your title _____

Step 6 Typing the paragraph

Type all the sentences you have written following paragraph format (see Appendix A).

パラグラフ・フォーマットに従って、ここまで書いた文をタイプしてみましょう。フォーマットについては、付録Aを参照してください。

Advanced

Add an introductory sentence (IS) before the topic sentence.

話題文の前に導入文を加えてみましょう。

> [IS1] We all have unique personalities.
> [IS2] Individuals are different in terms of personality.
> [IS3] Everyone has individual characteristics.
> [IS4] Nobody is identical in terms of personality.
> [IS5] Personalities among us are diverse.

Chapter 4 Revision
Describe Your Personality

We are at the revising stage. You will rewrite your first draft to make it more comprehensible.

修正の段階です。より分かりやすい文章になるようにファースト・ドラフトを書き換えてみます。

Step 1 Self-revision

Check your first draft with the checklist (see Appendix B).

付録Bのチェックリストを使って、ファースト・ドラフトを確認してください。

Step 2 Peer review

[Preparation]

(1) Type your individual sentences with extra space between the sentences.
(2) Cut them into strips. Each strip should have a single sentence (see the example below).

(1) 文と文の行間を十分にあけ、文をひとつずつタイプします。
(2) 文ごとに切り離します。ひとつの紙片にひとつの文とします（以下の例を参照）。

Individuals have unique characters.

✂--

My personality can best be described with three adjectives.

✂--

First, I am considerate.

✂--

Exchange your strips with a classmate. Put your partner's sentences in order. Leave aside any ones that you think do not fit in the paragraph.

クラスメートと紙片の束を交換します。パートナーの紙片を順番に並べてみてください。パラグラフのどこにも当てはまらないと思う文は横へ出しておきます。

Check your partner's order for your sentences.

並べてもらった紙片を確認してみましょう。

Step 3 Reorganizing the body : rewriting your main points and supporting sentences

Considering your partner's order for your sentences, rewrite your first draft. During revision, you should rethink the order of sentences, add and/or delete some sentences, and/or rephrase sentences. Also, ask your partner for his or her suggestions and comments.

先ほど並べてもらった順番を参考に、ファースト・ドラフトを書き直します。文の順番を変えたり、文を追加、あるいは削除したり、文を言い換えたりして修正していきます。また、パートナーに提案や意見を聞いてもよいでしょう。

Revising tips

[Introducing your main points]
When introducing the main points, the linking words *first*, *second*, and *finally* are most frequently used. You might also want to introduce the adjective you would like to emphasize the most as the first main point. See the examples below.

[メイン・ポイントの導入]
メイン・ポイントを導入するとき、first、second、finallyが最も頻繁に使われます。しかし、いつも同じ表現ではなく、工夫をしてみましょう。例えば、3つの形容詞から最も強調したいものを1番目に提示します。以下の例を参照してください。

---

1. First, I am opinionated.
2. First of all, I would describe myself as talkative.
3. The adjective honest should come first.
4. The first adjective that describes me is considerate.
5. The first adjective, competitive, describes my most outstanding characteristic.
6. First of all, the most noticeable characteristic is that I am positive.
7. The adjective ambitious is the one that describes me best.

Step 4 Rethinking and rewriting your topic sentence and concluding sentence

Rethink your topic and concluding sentences as well. Rewrite them if necessary.

話題文と結論文を再考してみましょう。必要であれば、書き直します。

【Revised topic sentence (書き直した話題文)】

_____

_____

【Revised concluding sentence (書き直した結論文)】

_____

_____

Step 5　Rethinking the title

Rethink the title. Is it clear and concrete enough for readers to guess the content of the paragraph? If not, you need to rewrite it.

タイトルを再考してみましょう。読者がパラグラフの内容を予測するために明確で具体的なタイトルになっていますか。そうでないと思ったら書き直しましょう。

【Revised title (書き直したタイトル)】

_____

Before the next class

Check your second draft with the checklist (see Appendix C) before you bring it to the next class.

次の授業にセカンド・ドラフトを持って行く前に、付録Cのチェックリストを使って、セカンド・ドラフトを確認してみましょう。

Peer review in class

Read and check a classmate's second draft, referring to the peer review sheet (see Appendix D).

クラスメートが書いたセカンド・ドラフトを、付録Dのピア・レビュー・シートに従って確認してみましょう。

Then, exchange comments on each other's paragraphs.

その後、お互いのパラグラフについてコメントをしてみましょう。

Chapter 5
Contrasting Two Countries

Chapter 5 focuses on contrasts between Japan and a foreign country. Compare the two countries and write about remarkable differences between them.

第5章では日本と外国の相違点を取りあげます。2つの国を比較して、注目すべき相違点について書いてみましょう。

Step 1 Brainstorming to generate ideas

▶ 【Sub-step 1】 Getting information

1. What countries are you interested in? Write down as many as you want.

   興味がある国はどこですか。できるだけたくさん書いてみましょう。

   _____

   _____

   _____

2. Choose the country you are interested in the most from the list of countries above.

   興味がある国の中から、最も興味がある国を選んでください。

   _____

3. Find some information about the country through an online search.

   その国についてオンラインで調べてみましょう。

Capital (首都)	
Population (人口)	
Size (面積)	
Official language(s) (公用語)	
Other information (その他の情報)	

Chapter 5 Contrasting Two Countries

4. What aspects of the country are you particularly interested in?
    Examples : food, fashion, college life, language, education, social welfare, religion

その国の特にどんなことに興味がありますか。
例：食べ物、ファッション、大学生の生活、ことば、教育、福祉、宗教

_____

_____

_____

▶ 【Sub-step 2】 Listing differences between the two countries

Compare Japan and another country in terms of the aspect you are interested in the most. You can use books and online research to collect information.

最も興味がある点について、日本ともうひとつの国を比較してみましょう。書籍やインターネットを使って情報を集めます。

日本	国名 [　　　　　　　　]

Step 2 Writing a topic sentence

Write a topic sentence (TS) after consulting the examples below. You should also add an organizational cue that tells how many main points you will have.

Write the name of the country you have chosen in the [ ] spaces and the aspect you have focused on for comparison in the underlined spaces (e.g., social welfare, food cultures, and education).

以下の例を参考にして、話題文を書いてみましょう。また、メイン・ポイントがいくつあるかを書くとパラグラフの構成が分かりやすくなります。

[ ]には国名、下線には比較のために焦点を当てた点（例えば社会福祉、食文化、教育）を書きます。

[TS1] Comparing [　　　　] and Japan, I found three interesting differences in terms of _____.
[TS2] Comparing [　　　　] and Japan, I was amazed at three remarkable differences regarding _____.
[TS3] Three interesting differences were found in _____ when comparing [　　　　] and Japan.
[TS4] A comparison of [　　　　] and Japan shows three interesting differences in terms of _____.
[TS5] A comparison of [　　　　] and Japan suggests that they are different in three ways regarding _____.

Write your topic sentence.

Step 3 Writing the body

▶ 【Sub-step 1】 Outlining main points

Choose three differences between the two countries that you would like to explain for the reader. Write a sentence that clearly explains each main point and includes an organizational cue.

Now, think about the order of the three differences. Instead of using

比較して分かった相違点の中から、ぜひ読者に伝えたい3点を選んでみましょう。そして、それぞれのメイン・ポイントを文にしてみましょう。その際、構成の手がかりとなる語句で始めると読者に分かりやすくなります。

では、3点の順番を考えてみましょう。今回はFirst、Second、Finallyではなく、興味深いと思う

Chapter 5 Contrasting Two Countries

First, *Second*, and *Finally*, order them depending on the degree of interest. In other words, write the most interesting difference first. You can see two example sentences for each main point below.

順で違いを紹介してみます。つまり、最も興味深いと思う違いを最初に書いてみましょう。以下に3つのメイン・ポイントがそれぞれ2つの例文で紹介されています。

1a. Most interestingly, they are different in terms of _____.

1b. The most interesting difference is that _____.

2a. Another interesting difference is _____.

2b. The next surprising difference is that _____.

3a. A final striking difference is that _____.

3b. An additional significant difference is that _____.

(形容詞 interestingと副詞 interestinglyをそれぞれamazing、amazingly、noticeable、noticeably、remarkable、remarkably、striking、strikinglyにしてもよい。)

▶ 【Sub-step 2】Writing supporting sentences

Explain your main points with supporting sentences. See how to show contrast below.

メイン・ポイントを説明するために支持文を書いてみましょう。相違の表し方は以下を参考にしてください。

Connecting two clauses

_____ while _____.

_____ whereas _____.

_____ although _____.

_____ ; on the other hand, _____.

_____ ; however, _____.

_____ ; in contrast _____.

_____ ; _____.

---

42 | Chapter 5 Contrasting Two Countries

Connecting two sentences

In contrast to Japan, _____.

Unlike Japan, _____.

However, _____.

On the other hand, _____.

[First main point (MP) and supporting sentences (SS)]

> [MP1] Most interestingly, these two countries are different in terms of table manners.
> [SS] Koreans leave their bowls and plates on the table when eating; on the other hand, Japanese lift them up and hold them in their hand when eating. Their table manners are totally opposite, and both groups believe that their own style is polite.

Write your first main point and supporting sentences.

_____

_____

_____

[Second main point and supporting sentences]

> [MP2] The next difference is the drinking age in the two countries.
> [SS] The legal drinking age in Germany is 16 whereas it is 20 in Japan. In other words, unlike Japan, even high school students can buy and drink alcohol in Germany.

Write your second main point and supporting sentences.

_____

_____

_____

[Third main point and supporting sentences]

[MP3] A final difference is when the first World Heritage site in each country was designated.
[SS] The first World Heritage site in Japan was announced in 1993; on the other hand, it was 10 years earlier in Spain, 1983. Since then, 17 and 44 sites have been named in Japan and Spain, respectively.

Write your third main point and supporting sentences.

_____

_____

_____

Step 4 Writing a concluding sentence

Write a concluding sentence (CS). The CS must be the rephrased TS starting with a linking phrase and including a listing of the three main points explained in the body. See the linking phrase box and example sentences below for reference. The underlined words indicate three differences mentioned in the body.

結論文を書いてみましょう。結論文はつなぎの語句から始まり、話題文を言い換えた文です。また、本文で触れた3つの相違点も書きます。以下のつなぎの語句と例文を参考にしてください。例文の下線部が本文で触れた3つの相違点を表しています。

Linking Phrase Box

> To sum up,
> In conclusion,
> As described above,
> As stated above,
> As explained above,

[CS1] In conclusion, Germany and Japan are different in terms of tax rates, education, and medical care.

44 | Chapter 5 Contrasting Two Countries

[CS2] To sum up, a comparison of Germany and Japan shows that they have different tax rates, educational systems, and medical care.
[CS3] As described above, China's and Japan's food cultures are different in terms of ingredients, cooking methods, and table manners.
[CS4] As stated above, Sweden and Japan are distinct from each other in college education : their term systems, their tuition rates, and the availability of scholarships.
[CS5] As explained above, a comparison of Spain and Japan shows interesting differences in terms of what time, where, and what they eat for lunch.

Step 5 Writing a title

Now, write a title for your paragraph. It should give a hint for readers to predict what the main point is in the paragraph.

では、ここまで書いた文章にタイトルをつけてみましょう。読む人が文章の内容を推測できるタイトルを考えます。

Your title _____

Step 6 Typing the paragraph

Type all the sentences you have written following paragraph format (see Appendix A).

パラグラフ・フォーマットに従って、ここまで書いた文をタイプしてみましょう。フォーマットについては、付録Aを参照してください。

Advanced

It may seem abrupt to the reader if a paragraph starts with a topic sentence without any introduction. In order to avoid an unexpected start, add an introductory sentence (IS) before the topic sentence.

パラグラフが話題文で始まっていると読者は唐突な感じがするかもしれません。こうした不意の始まりを避けるため、話題文の前に導入文を加えてみましょう。

[IS1] Culture influences various aspects of our daily life.
[IS2] Ways of thinking around the world are diverse.
[IS3] People in different countries have unique ideas about how to live.
[IS4] Watching sports is a popular entertainment throughout the world.
[IS5] Food cultures are diverse around the world.

Connecting sentences

Connect the introductory sentence and the topic sentence with a linking phrase, or add one more sentence to make them flow smoothly. See the examples below.

導入文と話題文がスムーズにつながるように、つなぎの語句や文を挿入してみましょう。以下の例を参考にしてください。

In the following examples : _____introductory sentence_____ ;
linking phrase/connecting sentence; _____topic sentence_____

Example 1

Culture influences various aspects of our daily life. Given this, when Brazil and Japan are compared, three interesting differences are found in terms of how they celebrate New Year's Day.

Example 2

Ways of thinking around the world are diverse. As a result, even two countries in Asia differ from each other. Comparing Korea and Japan, there are three remarkable differences regarding table manners.

Example 3

People in different countries have unique ideas about how to live. Following this view, Germany and Japan are not exceptions : a comparison of the two countries reveals three interesting differences in terms of their style of living.

Example 4

Watching sports is a popular entertainment throughout the world. However, nations seem to prefer different sports. Given this, there are three interesting differences between the U.S. and Japan.
OR
Watching sports is a popular entertainment throughout the world. Given this, there are three interesting differences between the U.S. and Japan.

Example 5

Food cultures are diverse around the world. Accordingly, comparing China and Japan shows three noticeable differences between them.

Chapter 6 Revision
Contrasting Two Countries

We are at the revising stage. You will rewrite your first draft to make it more comprehensible.

修正の段階です。より分かりやすい文章になるようにファースト・ドラフトを書き換えてみます。

Step 1 Self-revision

Check your first draft with the checklist (see Appendix B).

付録Bのチェックリストを使って、ファースト・ドラフトを確認してください。

Step 2 Peer review

[Preparation]
(1) Type your individual sentences with extra space between the sentences.
(2) Cut them into strips. Each strip should have a single sentence.

（1）文と文の行間を十分にあけ、文をひとつずつタイプします。
（2）文ごとに切り離します。ひとつの紙片にひとつの文とします。

Exchange your strips with a classmate. Put your partner's sentences in order. Leave aside any ones you think do not fit in the paragraph.

クラスメートと紙片の束を交換します。パートナーの紙片を順番に並べてみてください。パラグラフのどこにも当てはまらないと思う文は横へ出しておきます。

Check your partner's order for your sentences.

並べてもらった紙片を確認してみましょう。

Step 3 Reorganizing the body : rewriting your main points and supporting sentences

Considering your partner's order for your sentences, rewrite your first draft. During revision, you should rethink the order of your sentences, add and/or delete some sentences, and/or rephrase sentences. Also, ask your partner for his or her suggestions and comments.

先ほど並べてもらった順番を参考に、ファースト・ドラフトを書き直します。文の順番を変えたり、文を追加、あるいは削除したり、文を言い換えたりして修正していきます。また、パートナーに提案や意見を聞いてもよいでしょう。

Step 4 Rethinking and rewriting your topic sentence and concluding sentence

Rethink your topic and concluding sentences as well. Rewrite them if necessary.

話題文と結論文を再考してみましょう。必要であれば、書き直します。

【Revised topic sentence（書き直した話題文）】

_____

_____

【Revised concluding sentence（書き直した結論文）】

_____

_____

Step 5 Rethinking the title

Rethink the title. Is it clear and concrete enough for readers to guess the content of the paragraph? If not, you need to rewrite it.

タイトルを再考してみましょう。読者がパラグラフの内容を予測するために明確で具体的なタイトルになっていますか。そうでないと思ったら書き直しましょう。

【Revised title（書き直したタイトル）】

_____

Before the next class

Check your second draft with the checklist (see Appendix C) before you bring it to the next class.

次の授業にセカンド・ドラフトを持って行く前に、付録Cのチェックリストを使って、セカンド・ドラフトを確認してみましょう。

Peer review in class

Read and check a classmate's second draft, referring to the peer review sheet (see Appendix D).

クラスメートが書いたセカンド・ドラフトを、付録Dのピア・レビュー・シートに従って確認してみましょう。

Then, exchange comments on each other's paragraphs.

その後、お互いのパラグラフについてコメントをしてみましょう。

Chapter 7
Analyzing Reasons & Results

Chapter 7 focuses on reasons and results. You will explain a health issue by giving reasons and results.

第7章では理由と結果に焦点を当てます。健康について取りあげ、理由と結果を説明してみましょう。

Step 1   Brainstorming to generate ideas

▶ 【Sub-step 1】 Exploring ideas through answering questions

Three topics are suggested below. Each has four questions. They should help you brainstorm and decide on a topic for writing.

以下に3つのトピックが提案されています。それぞれのトピックに質問が4つあります。質問に回答することでブレイン・ストーミングが行いやすくなり、トピックを決めるために役に立ちます。

Suggested Topic 1

a. Do you eat breakfast every day?

毎日、朝食を食べますか。

_____

_____

b. Why do some people skip breakfast?

朝食を抜いてしまう原因は何でしょうか。

_____

_____

c. Why should we eat breakfast?

なぜ朝食を食べたほうがよいのでしょうか。

_____

_____

d. What happens if we skip breakfast?

朝食を抜くとどのような結果をもたらすのでしょうか。

_____

_____

Suggested Topic 2

a. Do you get moderate exercise?

適度な運動をしていますか。

b. What are the merits of moderate exercise for us?

適度な運動をするメリットは何でしょうか。

c. What are the reasons for a lack of exercise?

なぜ運動不足になるのでしょうか。

d. What does lack of exercise cause?

運動不足はどのような結果をもたらすのでしょうか。

Suggested Topic 3

a. How long is an ideal night's sleep?

   何時間の睡眠が理想なのでしょうか。

b. Why do we need a sufficient amount of sleep?

   なぜ十分な睡眠は必要なのでしょうか。

c. What causes lack of sleep?

   なぜ睡眠不足になるのでしょうか。

d. What happens if we do not sleep enough?

   睡眠不足はどのような結果をもたらすのでしょうか。

Other possible topics : overeating, eating junk food, smoking, excessive drinking, excessive dieting

▶ 【Sub-step 2】 Exploring the topic through an online search

Search online to collect scientific and medical information for the topic you have chosen.

決定したトピックについて科学的または医学的な情報をオンラインで検索してみましょう。

Chapter 7 Analyzing Reasons & Results | 55

MEMO

Step 2 Writing a topic sentence

Write a topic sentence (TS) after consulting the examples below. You should also add an organizational cue that tells how many main points you will have.

以下の例を参考にして、話題文を書いてみましょう。また、メイン・ポイントがいくつあるかを書くとパラグラフの構成が分かりやすくなります。

[TS1] There are two major positive effects of eating breakfast.
[TS2] Not eating breakfast has two major negative effects on our health.
[TS3] Regular exercise has two positive effects.
[TS4] There are two serious problems caused by lack of exercise.
[TS5] Getting sufficient sleep is necessary since it has two positive effects.
[TS6] Lack of sleep increases the risk of being sick in two ways.

Write your topic sentence.

Step 3 Writing an introductory sentence

It may seem abrupt to the reader if a paragraph starts with a topic sentence without any introduction. In order to avoid an unexpected start, add an introductory sentence (IS) before the topic sentence.

パラグラフが話題文で始まっていると読者は唐突な感じがするかもしれません。こうした不意の始まりを避けるため、話題文の前に導入文を加えてみましょう。

[IS1] Nowadays, many young people skip breakfast.
[IS2] Eating breakfast is necessary for us to stay healthy.
[IS3] Many people tend to neglect exercise routines in order to finish their work.
[IS4] Recently, many people are too busy to exercise regularly.
[IS5] The modern lifestyle gives us too many opportunities to stay up late.
[IS6] We often reduce our sleeping hours because of our busy schedule.

Advanced

[IS7] Some people tend to skip eating breakfast due to their busy schedule.
[IS8] Many people tend to neglect exercise routines in order to finish their work.
[IS9] Modern people tend to neglect one of the fundamental daily activities, sleeping.

Connecting sentences

Connect the introductory sentence and the topic sentence with a linking phrase, or add one more sentence to make them flow smoothly. See the examples below.

導入文と話題文がスムーズにつながるように、つなぎの語句や文を挿入してみましょう。以下の例を参考にしてください。

In the following examples : _____introductory sentence_____ ; linking phrase/connecting sentence; _____topic sentence_____

Example 1

Nowadays, many young people do not have breakfast. This is not a good idea, particularly for students. There are two major positive effects of eating breakfast.

Example 2

Eating breakfast is necessary for us to stay healthy. There is a strong relationship between breakfast and health. Therefore, not eating breakfast has two major negative effects on our health.

Example 3

Many people tend to neglect exercise routines in order to finish their work. However, doctors suggest that we should exercise at least three times a week. If we follow their advice, regular exercise has two positive effects.

Example 4

Recently, many people are too busy to exercise regularly. This leads to a lack of exercise and eventually health problems. In particular, there are two serious problems caused by lack of exercise.

Example 5

The modern lifestyle gives us too many opportunities to stay up late. As a result, we often neglect a routine daily activity, sleeping. However, getting sufficient sleep is necessary since it has two positive effects.

Example 6

We often reduce our sleeping hours because of our busy schedule. However, lack of sleep increases the risk of being sick in two ways.

Write your introductory and topic sentences with a linking phrase/connecting sentence.

_____

_____

_____

_____

Step 4　Writing the body

▶【Sub-step 1】Outlining main points

Choose two major findings out of those you have found through your online search that you would like readers to know about the topic. Write a sentence that clearly explains each main point and includes an organizational cue. You can see two example sentences for each main point on the next page for reference. The first and second sets of sentences show positive and negative points respectively.	まず、オンラインで調べて分かったことがらのうち、読者に伝えたい主要な発見を2つ選んでみましょう。そして、それらをメイン・ポイントとして本文で説明をします。その際、文章構成を示す語句で始めると読者に分かりやすくなります。次頁にそれぞれのメイン・ポイントの書き出しが紹介されています。1aと1bの書き出しはよい点、2aと2bは問題点について書かれることを示しています。

1a. The first merit/effect/benefit is _____.

1b. The next merit/effect/benefit is _____.

2a. The first serious problem is _____.

2b. Another serious problem is _____.

Write your first main point.

_____

_____

Write your second main point.

_____

_____

▶ 【Sub-step 2】 **Writing supporting sentences**

Explain your main points with supporting sentences. There are three examples for each main point below.

メイン・ポイントを説明するために支持文を書いてみましょう。各々のメイン・ポイントに3つの例が提示してあります。

[First main point & explanation]

Example 1

[MP1] The most serious problem is a risk of gaining weight.

[Supporting sentences to explain MP1]
Without breakfast, people's biorhythm is affected, and the metabolism of energy is not efficient. In addition, they tend to overeat and have snacks. Because of these factors, extra calories are stored as body fat.

Example 2

> [MP1] The first major benefit is that regular exercise promotes positive feelings.
>
> [Supporting sentences to explain MP1]
> Physical activity increases the brain chemicals that make you feel happy and relaxed. You can gain self-confidence in your appearance and toward your work through regular exercise.

Example 3

> [MP1] The first major effect is that sufficient sleep improves our immunity.
>
> [Supporting sentences to explain MP1]
> While sleeping, the sympathetic nerve is weakened and the parasympathetic nerve is activated. A good balance between the two nerves is necessary to increase our immune strength. Immune strength is very important in preventing us from getting sick.

Write your supporting sentences for your first main point.

_____

_____

_____

_____

[Second main point & explanation]

Example 4

> [MP2] The next merit is that eating breakfast improves academic performance.
>
> [Supporting sentences to explain MP2]
> Students who eat breakfast can focus and are prepared to learn; on the other hand, without breakfast, students are too hungry to be motivated to learn. This suggests that eating breakfast creates a positive learning environment.

Example 5

[MP2] Another serious problem is that lack of exercise hastens the aging process.

[Supporting sentences to explain MP2]
As we get older, muscle size decreases. This physical phenomenon decreases the amount of amino acids, which destroy germs and weakens the heart. However, aging is not the primary reason for smaller muscles. Rather, lack of exercise is.

Example 6

[MP2] Another health problem is that lack of sleep increases the chance of developing chronic depression.

[Supporting sentences to explain MP2]
People without enough sleep tend to easily feel down, be mentally unstable, and lose confidence. These phenomena are warning signs of mental problems.

Write your supporting sentences for your second main point.

_____

_____

_____

_____

_____

Step 5 Writing a concluding sentence

Write a concluding sentence (CS). The CS must be the rephrased TS starting with a linking phrase. See the linking phrase box and example sentences below for reference.

結論文を書いてみましょう。結論文はつなぎの語句から始まり、話題文を言い換えた文です。以下のつなぎの語句と例文を参考にしてください。

Linking Phrase Box

> To sum up,
> In conclusion,
> As described above,
> As stated above,
> As explained above,

[CS1] To sum up, eating breakfast has two benefits: it increases concentration and improves academic performance.
[CS2] As stated above, not eating breakfast negatively affects our daily life by causing a lack of concentration and weight gain.
[CS3] In conclusion, the two main benefits of moderate exercise are getting in shape and releasing stress.
[CS4] As explained above, two major problems caused by lack of exercise are gaining weight and advancing the aging process.
[CS5] To sum up, two advantages of sufficient sleep are increasing immune strength and lowering the chance of gaining weight.
[CS6] As described above, lack of sleep puts our physical and mental health in danger, causing life-related diseases and depression.

Step 6 Writing a title

Now, write a title for your paragraph. It should give a hint for readers to predict what the main point is in the paragraph.

では、ここまで書いた文章にタイトルをつけてみましょう。読む人が文章の内容を推測できるタイトルを考えます。

Your title _____

Step 7   Typing the paragraph

Type all the sentences you have written following paragraph format (see Appendix A).

パラグラフ・フォーマットに従って、ここまで書いた文をタイプしてみましょう。フォーマットについては、付録Aを参照してください。

Advanced

Add a final thought/comment to the concluding sentence in order to end the paragraph.

結論文の後に一言加えてパラグラフを終了してみましょう。

[FT1] Therefore, breakfast is the most important meal of the day.
[FT2] Now, I hope you want to spend an extra ten minutes eating breakfast instead of staying in bed.
[FT3] Now, you know that regular exercise does not mean every day.
[FT4] In order to prevent these problems, moderate exercise is recommended.
[FT5] Experts recommend that the ideal amount of sleep is six to seven hours per night.
[FT6] Thus, in order to survive a busy life, sufficient sleep is a key.

Write your final thought or comment.

Chapter 8 Revision
Analyzing Reasons & Results

We are at the revising stage. You will rewrite your first draft to make it more comprehensible.

修正の段階です。より分かりやすい文章になるようにファースト・ドラフトを書き換えてみます。

Step 1 Self-revision

Check your first draft with the checklist (see Appendix B).

付録Bのチェックリストを使って、ファースト・ドラフトを確認してください。

Step 2 Peer review

[Preparation]
(1) Type your individual sentences with extra space between the sentences.
(2) Cut them into strips. Each strip should have a single sentence.

（1）文と文の行間を十分にあけ、文をひとつずつタイプします。
（2）文ごとに切り離します。ひとつの紙片にひとつの文とします。

Exchange your strips with a classmate. Put your partner's sentences in order. Leave aside any ones you think do not fit in the paragraph.

クラスメートと紙片の束を交換します。パートナーの紙片を順番に並べてみてください。パラグラフのどこにも当てはまらないと思う文は横へ出しておきます。

Check your partner's order for your sentences.

並べてもらった紙片を確認してみましょう。

Step 3 Reorganizing the body : rewriting your main points and supporting sentences

Considering your partner's order for your sentences, rewrite your first draft. During revision, you should rethink the order of your sentences, add and/or delete some sentences, and/or rephrase sentences. Also, ask your partner for his or her suggestions and comments.

先ほど並べてもらった順番を参考に、ファースト・ドラフトを書き直します。文の順番を変えたり、文を追加、あるいは削除したり、文を言い換えたりして修正していきます。また、パートナーに提案や意見を聞いてもよいでしょう。

Step 4 Rethinking and rewriting your topic sentence and concluding sentence

Rethink your topic and concluding sentences as well. Rewrite them if necessary.

話題文と結論文を再考してみましょう。必要であれば、書き直します。

【Revised topic sentence（書き直した話題文）】

_____

_____

【Revised concluding sentence（書き直した結論文）】

_____

_____

Step 5　Rethinking the title

Rethink the title. Is it clear and concrete enough for readers to guess the content of the paragraph? If not, you need to rewrite it.	タイトルを再考してみましょう。読者がパラグラフの内容を予測するために明確で具体的なタイトルになっていますか。そうでないと思ったら書き直しましょう。

【Revised title（書き直したタイトル）】

_____

Before the next class

Check your second draft with the checklist (see Appendix C) before you bring it to the next class.	次の授業にセカンド・ドラフトを持って行く前に、付録Cのチェックリストを使って、セカンド・ドラフトを確認してみましょう。

Peer review in class

Read and check a classmate's second draft, referring to the peer review sheet (see Appendix D).	クラスメートが書いたセカンド・ドラフトを、付録Dのピア・レビュー・シートに従って確認してみましょう。
Then, exchange comments on each other's paragraphs.	その後、お互いのパラグラフについてコメントをしてみましょう。

Chapter 9
Giving Suggestion

Chapter 9 focuses on how to give a suggestion for a particular problem. You will provide a possible solution to a problem that concerns you in your daily life, explaining why you think it will work and what benefits it will have.

第9章では問題解決に焦点を当てます。日常生活で直面する問題を取りあげ、解決策を提案してみましょう。また、なぜその解決策が有効だと思うか、どのような利点があるかをも合わせて説明します。

Step 1 Exploring possible topics

Four topics are suggested below. Each has two questions. Think about them, and then choose the topic you are interested in the most.

以下に４つのトピックが提案されています。それぞれのトピックに質問が２つあります。それらを考えてから、最も面白いと思うトピックを選んでみましょう。

Suggested Topic 1

Some students cheat on examinations. Undoubtedly, this is misconduct.

試験でカンニングをする学生がいます。明らかにこれは誤った行為です。

① Why do they cheat?

なぜ、学生はカンニングをするのでしょうか。

_____
_____

② What solutions can you think of in order to prevent their cheating?

学生のカンニングを防ぐために、どのような解決策が考えられますか。

_____
_____

Suggested Topic 2

Some people smoke in restaurants. This behavior often annoys others, in particular those who do not smoke.

レストランでタバコを吸う人がいます。この行いは、しばしば他人、特にタバコを吸わない人には迷惑です。

① What harmful effects do you think smoking in restaurants has?

レストランで喫煙することにより、どのような弊害が考えられますか。

_____
_____

② What solutions can you think of in order for both smokers and non-smokers to enjoy their meals in comfort at restaurants?

タバコを吸う人も吸わない人もお互い気持ちよく食事をするために、どのような解決策が考えられますか。

___

___

Suggested Topic 3

Many people listen to music on the train. We often overhear their music leaking from their headphones or earphones. Those sounds irritate others on the train.

電車の中で音楽を聴いている人がたくさんいます。そういう人たちの近くにいるとヘッドフォンやイヤホンから音楽が漏れて聞こえてくることがよくあります。乗客の中にはこの音にイライラする人もいます。

① Why does their music leak from their headphones or earphones?

なぜ、ヘッドフォンやイヤホンから音楽が漏れるのでしょうか。

___

___

② What solutions can you think of?

どのような解決策が考えられますか。

___

___

Suggested Topic 4

Some people stare at their smartphone screen while walking or riding a bicycle. Their behavior is very dangerous.

スマートフォンのスクリーンを見ながら道を歩いている人や、自転車に乗っている人がいます。このような行為は大変危険です。

① What problems might happen if people stare at their smartphone screen while walking or riding a bicycle?

スマートフォンのスクリーンを見ながら歩いたり自転車に乗ったりすると、どのような危険がありますか。

_____

_____

② What solutions can you think of in order to discourage this behavior?

このような行為を減らすために、どのような解決策が考えられますか。

_____

_____

Step 2　Brainstorming to generate ideas through group discussion

Choose the topic you are interested in the most. Make a group of four who have chosen the same topic and share your ideas.

最も興味があるトピックをひとつ選びます。そして、同じトピックを選んだ4名でグループを作り、意見交換をしてみましょう。

Your topic : _____

Step 3　Outlining

Write an outline of your paragraph by answering the questions on the next page.

次頁の質問に答えて、パラグラフのアウトラインを書いてみましょう。

Introduction : What problem are you describing?　　［取りあげる問題点］

_____

_____

▼

Topic sentence : What is a possible solution?　　［どのような解決策があるか］

_____

_____

▼

Supporting sentences :
Why do you suggest this particular solution?　　［なぜその解決策を提案するのか］
How would you implement it?　　［具体的にどのような方法で実行するか］
What benefits does the solution bring?　　［解決策がもたらす利点は何か］

_____

_____

_____

Step 4　Writing an introductory sentence, problem, and solution

Write sentences to introduce your theme, explain the problem, and suggest a possible solution after consulting the examples below. ： パラグラフのテーマを紹介して、取りあげる問題点を説明し、そして可能な解決策を提案します。例を参考にして、これらを書いてみましょう。

Sample sentences to introduce a theme

> 1. Some people believe that their misbehavior is not such a big deal.
> 2. Some people are not aware that their behavior is serious misconduct.
> 3. One person's behavior can be a problem for others.
> 4. Ways of thinking and behaving are very diverse.
> 5. Everyone should be equally comfortable in public places, including trains.
> 6. We often forget that people feel and behave differently.
> 7. We may not all share the same ideas about how to behave in public.
> 8. We must consider others in public, where everyone shares a common space.

Sample sentences to describe a problem

1. Some college students do not know that cheating is serious misconduct.
2. College students may think that cheating is not such a big deal.
3. Smoking in restaurants is a behavior that some people consider a problem.
4. People react differently to smoking in a restaurant.
5. We often overhear the sound from someone else's headphones.
6. Listening to music on a train entertains some people and bothers others.
7. It is often annoying to others when people stare at their smartphone screens while walking or riding a bicycle.
8. Many people play with their smartphone while walking or even riding a bike.

Sample sentences to describe a possible solution (= topic sentence)

1. In order to promote their awareness of the problem, universities should inform students that they will experience very severe consequences as a result of cheating.
2. In order to prevent cheating, exams should be designed to measure students' ability to think logically by applying what they have learned in a course, not their ability to transfer knowledge to a piece of exam paper.
3. In order for everyone to equally enjoy their meal, smoking should be prohibited in all restaurants.
4. In order for everyone to enjoy their meal at a restaurant, smoking should be restricted to only limited places.
5. Train companies should actively conduct campaigns to promote public awareness of this issue.
6. In order for everyone to spend a pleasant time, quiet-zone train cars should be designated.
7. In order for everyone to walk safely, those who use a smartphone on the road should be fined.
8. In order to avoid accidents, companies should invent smartphones that automatically lock when the user is walking or riding a bike.

Connecting sentences

It is important to pay attention to how to connect sentences. You can make them flow smoothly with a linking phrase.

文と文のつながりを考えることが大切です。前後の文がスムーズにつながるように、つなぎの語句を挿入してみましょう。

In the following examples, ▧▧▧▧ indicates a connecting word or phrase.

Example 1

| Introducing a theme | Some people believe that their misbehavior is not such a big deal. |

| Problem | Consequently/As a result, some college students do not know that cheating is serious misconduct. |

| Possible solution (topic sentence) | In order to promote their awareness of the problem, universities should inform students that they will experience very severe consequences as a result of cheating. |

Example 2

| Introducing a theme | Some people are not aware that their behavior is serious misconduct. |

| Problem | For example,/Thus, college students may think that cheating is not such a big deal. |

| Possible solution (topic sentence) | In order to prevent cheating, exams should be designed to measure students' ability to think logically by applying what they have learned in a course, not their ability to transfer knowledge to a piece of exam paper. |

Example 3

| Introducing a theme | One person's behavior can be a problem for others. |

| Problem | Smoking in restaurants is a behavior that some people consider a problem. |

| Possible solution (topic sentence) | In order for everyone to equally enjoy their meal, smoking should be prohibited in all restaurants. |

Example 4

Introducing a theme	Ways of thinking and behaving are very diverse.
Problem	As a result, people react differently to smoking in a restaurant.
Possible solution (topic sentence)	In order for everyone to enjoy their meal at a restaurant, smoking should be restricted to only limited places.

Example 5

Introducing a theme	Everyone should be equally comfortable in public places, including trains.
Problem	However, we often overhear the sound from someone else's headphones.
Possible solution (topic sentence)	Train companies should actively conduct campaigns to promote public awareness of this issue.

Example 6

Introducing a theme	We often forget that people feel and behave differently.
Problem	For example, listening to music on a train entertains some people and bothers others.
Possible solution (topic sentence)	In order for everyone to spend a pleasant time, quiet-zone train cars should be designated.

Example 7

Introducing a theme	We may not all share the same ideas about how to behave in public.
Problem	For example, it is often annoying to others when people stare at their smartphone screens while walking or riding a bicycle.
Possible solution (topic sentence)	In order for everyone to walk safely, those who use a smartphone on the road should be fined.

Example 8

Introducing a theme	We must consider others in public, where everyone shares a common space.
Problem	Unfortunately, many people play with their smartphone while walking or even riding a bike.
Possible solution (topic sentence)	In order to avoid accidents, companies should invent smartphones that automatically lock when the user is walking or riding a bike.

Write your sentences to introduce the theme, explain the problem, and suggest a possible solution.

_____
_____
_____
_____
_____

Step 5 Writing supporting sentences

In order to support your solution (topic sentence), explain why you suggest it, how you can implement it, and what benefits it has for people.

解決策（話題文）を支持するために、なぜその解決策を提案するのか、どのように実行するのか、どのような利点をもたらすのかを説明してみましょう。

Why do you suggest your particular solution? [なぜ、その解決策を提案するのか]

> [1a] Students underestimate the seriousness of cheating. If they get caught, they will be in a difficult situation : they will automatically fail all their courses.
> [2a] As long as they sit in a classroom to take exams, they will try to come up with better ways to cheat. This pattern will be endless.
> [3a] Cigarette smoke and its smell ruin the taste of food. People go to a restaurant to enjoy good food. Their desire must be respected.
> [4a] We need to respect both smokers' and non-smokers' rights. Smokers want to smoke while non-smokers want to enjoy their meals.

[5a] Some passengers may not realize that their music is being overheard through their headphones. Therefore, it is necessary to teach them that it bothers others.

[6a] It is difficult for some people to understand that passengers around them are annoyed by their music. Thus, designated train cars should meet both sides' desires.

[7a] Since their behavior increases the chance of a traffic accident, it should be considered a traffic violation.

[8a] Since they do not pay attention to people and things happening around them, their reactions are not as fast as they think. For this reason, their behavior will cause accidents.

Write your sentences to explain the reason for your suggestion.

How would you implement it? [どのように実行するか]

[1b] The university should give freshmen a brochure that warns about cheating at the entrance ceremony. From the very beginning, they need to know that they will pay for misbehavior.

[2b] Students should be given a week to write a take-home exam. In order to finish it, they must put together everything they have learned during the term and do online and library research.

[3b] A sign should be put up with an explanation of why smoking is prohibited at the restaurant : food is tastier in a smoke-free environment than with cigarette smoke.

[4b] Restaurants can be separated into two sections, smoking and non-smoking areas. Then, ashtrays should be removed from non-smoking areas.

[5b] Train companies should put up posters in stations and on trains to make sure passengers are aware that not everyone enjoys musical sounds on the train.

[6b] Those who enjoy listening to music and those who do not can be in different train cars. Passengers in the quiet-zone cars will not be allowed to do any music listening.

[7b] It should be illegal for people to play with a smartphone while walking or riding a bicycle; they should be fined if they get caught.

[8b] The smartphone should automatically shut down once it senses the motion of a user walking or riding a bicycle.

Write your sentences to explain how to implement your suggestion.

_____

_____

_____

_____

_____

What benefits does the solution have? [解決策がもたらす利点は何か]

[1c]	Awareness of the severe consequences should discourage students from cheating on tests.
[2c]	Take-home exams will promote critical thinking by students.
[3c/4c]	More non-smokers will appreciate the consideration for them and choose the smoke-free restaurants.
[3c/4c]	The suggested solution would also have a positive effect on non-smoking employees. They will be as happy as the customers and enjoy working there. Their positive attitude should lead to better service for customers.
[5c]	Reading the posters, some passengers will notice that their behavior may bother others.
[6c]	Passengers who do not enjoy music can have a pleasant ride without hearing annoying sounds.
[7c]	Once they realize that their behavior is legally misconduct, they will be reluctant to play with a smartphone while walking or riding a bicycle.
[7c']	Such legal force should definitely discourage them from playing with a smartphone while walking or riding a bicycle.
[8c]	If the smartphone repeatedly shuts down every time they try to play with it while walking or riding a bicycle, they will get used to not trying to use it in some public places.

Write your sentences to explain the benefits that your suggested solution will have.

_____
_____
_____
_____

Step 6 Writing a concluding sentence

Write a concluding sentence (CS). Remember that you must rephrase the topic sentence and should not add any new ideas. See the linking phrase box and example sentences below for your reference.

結論文を書いてみましょう。結論文は話題文を言い換えるだけで、新しいことは書きません。以下のつなぎの語句と例を参考にしてください。

Linking Phrase Box

> In conclusion,
> As explained above,
> As suggested above,

[CS1] As explained above, clear instructions should discourage students from cheating; knowing how severely they will be punished as a consequence will be effective.

[CS2] As suggested above, giving take-home exams would be one solution to discourage students from cheating on tests.

[CS3] In conclusion, smoking should be prohibited in restaurants so that everyone can have a good time.

[CS4] As explained above, restaurants should allow smokers to smoke only in restricted places.

[CS5] As suggested above, posters at stations and on trains should promote passengers' awareness of noise problems.

[CS6] In conclusion, creating quiet-zone train cars would be one solution for those who do not enjoy annoying sounds from someone else's headphones.

[CS7] In conclusion, those who use a smartphone on the street should pay for their misbehavior.

[CS8] As explained above, equipping smartphones with an automatic shutdown function is one possible solution to avoid traffic accidents.

Write your concluding sentence.

_____

_____

Step 7   Writing a title

| Now, write a title for your paragraph. It should give a hint for readers to predict what the main point is in the paragraph. | では、ここまで書いた文章にタイトルをつけてみましょう。読む人が文章の内容を推測できるタイトルを考えます。 |

Your title _____

Step 8   Typing the paragraph

| Type all the sentences you have written following paragraph format (see Appendix A). | パラグラフ・フォーマットに従って、ここまで書いた文をタイプしてみましょう。フォーマットについては、付録Aを参照してください。 |

Chapter 10 Revision
Giving Suggestion

We are at the revising stage. You will rewrite your first draft to make it more comprehensible.

修正の段階です。より分かりやすい文章になるようにファースト・ドラフトを書き換えてみます。

Step 1 Self-revision

Check your first draft with the checklist (see Appendix B).

付録Bのチェックリストを使って、ファースト・ドラフトを確認してください。

Step 2 Peer review

[Preparation]
(1) Type your individual sentences with extra space between the sentences.
(2) Cut them into strips. Each strip should have a single sentence.

（1）文と文の行間を十分にあけ、文をひとつずつタイプします。
（2）文ごとに切り離します。ひとつの紙片にひとつの文とします。

Exchange your strips with a classmate. Put your partner's sentences in order. Leave aside any ones you think do not fit in the paragraph.

クラスメートと紙片の束を交換します。パートナーの紙片を順番に並べてみてください。パラグラフのどこにも当てはまらないと思う文は横へ出しておきます。

Check your partner's order for your sentences.

並べてもらった紙片を確認してみましょう。

Step 3 Reorganizing the body : rewriting your main points and supporting sentences

Considering your partner's order for your sentences, rewrite your first draft. During revision, you should rethink the order of your sentences, add and/or delete some sentences, and/or rephrase sentences. Also, ask your partner for his or her suggestions and comments.

先ほど並べてもらった順番を参考に、ファースト・ドラフトを書き直します。文の順番を変えたり、文を追加、あるいは削除したり、文を言い換えたりして修正していきます。また、パートナーに提案や意見を聞いてもよいでしょう。

Step 4 Rethinking and rewriting your topic sentence and concluding sentence

Rethink your topic and concluding sentences as well. Rewrite them if necessary.

話題文と結論文を再考してみましょう。必要であれば、書き直します。

【Revised topic sentence（書き直した話題文）】

【Revised concluding sentence（書き直した結論文）】

Step 5　Rethinking the title

Rethink the title. Is it clear and concrete enough for readers to guess the content of the paragraph? If not, you need to rewrite it.

タイトルを再考してみましょう。読者がパラグラフの内容を予測するために明確で具体的なタイトルになっていますか。そうでないと思ったら書き直しましょう。

【Revised title（書き直したタイトル）】

Before the next class

Check your second draft with the checklist (see Appendix C) before you bring it to the next class.

次の授業にセカンド・ドラフトを持って行く前に、付録Cのチェックリストを使って、セカンド・ドラフトを確認してみましょう。

Peer review in class

Read and check a classmate's second draft, referring to the peer review sheet (see Appendix D).

クラスメートが書いたセカンド・ドラフトを、付録Dのピア・レビュー・シートに従って確認してみましょう。

Then, exchange comments on each other's paragraphs.

その後、お互いのパラグラフについてコメントをしてみましょう。

Chapter 11
Stating Your Opinion

Chapter 11 focuses on how to express an opinion. You must support your opinion with a logical and persuasive explanation to convince readers.

第11章では意見の述べ方に焦点を当てます。読者に納得してもらうために、論理的で説得力のある説明をすることで自分の意見をサポートします。

Step 1　Exploring possible topics

Four topics are suggested below. Each has three questions. Think about them, and then choose the topic you are interested in the most.

以下に４つのトピックが提案されています。それぞれのトピックに質問が３つあります。それらを考えてから、最も面白いと思うトピックを選んでみましょう。

Suggested Topic 1

Everyone should learn English as a lingua franca.

みんなが英語をリンガ・フランカとして学ぶべきである。

① What is the definition of a lingua franca?

　リンガ・フランカはどのように定義されていますか。

_____

_____

② What are the merits of learning English?

　英語を学習するメリットは何だと思いますか。

_____

_____

③ What are the merits and demerits for people around the world to speak English?

　世界の人びとが英語を話すメリットとデメリットは何だと思いますか。

_____

_____

Suggested Topic 2

Young Japanese should go abroad in this era of globalization.

グローバル時代の今、日本の若者は海外へ行くべきである。

① What countries or areas do you think of when you hear "abroad" or "overseas"?

あなたにとって「海外」とは具体的にどこの国や地域を指しますか。

_____

_____

② What do you think that "this era of globalization" means?

「グローバル時代」「グローバライゼーションの時代」とは何を意味すると思いますか。

_____

_____

③ What do you think are the merits and demerits of young people going abroad?

若者が海外へ行くメリットとデメリットは何だと思いますか。

_____

_____

Suggested Topic 3

Social networking services (SNS) such as Facebook and LINE are the ideal communication tool for everyone.

フェイスブックやLINEなどのSNSは理想的なコミュニケーションの道具である。

① Do you use any SNS? If your answer is yes, when do you use them? If your answer is no, why don't you use them?

SNSを利用していますか。「はい」の場合、いつSNSを使いますか。「いいえ」の場合、なぜSNSを使いませんか。

_____

_____

② What are the merits of using SNS?

SNSを使うメリットは何だと思いますか。

_____

③ What problems do you think the use of SNS causes?

SNSを使うことでどのような問題が生じると思いますか。

Suggested Topic 4

We should accept foreigners as nursing-care workers in Japan.

日本で外国人を介護福祉士として受け入れるべきである。

① What are the merits of admitting foreigners into Japan as nursing-care workers?

外国人を介護福祉士として日本へ受け入れるメリットとは何だと思いますか。

② What issues do we need to be concerned about when bringing foreigners into Japan as nursing-care workers?

外国人を介護福祉士として日本へ受け入れる際、どのような課題を考えなければなりませんか。

③ What would be the effect in the future of increasing the number of foreigners who are permitted to enter Japan as nursing-care workers?

介護福祉士として今後外国人が増えることで、日本の社会にどのような影響があると考えられますか。

Step 2 Online search & group discussion

▶ 【Sub-step 1】 Online search

Choose one of the four possible topics above. Do an online search and collect some information related to the topic you have chosen. Then, think about the accompanying questions to explore the topic again.

先ほどの4つのトピックからひとつ選びます。それについてオンラインで関連する情報を集め、再度質問を考えてみましょう。

▶ 【Sub-step 2】 Group discussion

Make a group of four who are interested in the same topic. Share your ideas about the topic that you have explored based on the information from your online search.

同じトピックに興味を持つ4名でグループを作って、オンライン・サーチで集めた情報をもとに意見交換をしてみましょう。

▶ 【Sub-step 3】 Decide on your position :

Do you agree or disagree with the suggested topic statement listed above? Considering the ideas of the others in your group as well as your own, decide whether you agree or disagree with the topic statement.

上で提案されているトピックの意見に賛成ですか、反対ですか。グループの意見も考慮しながら、自分の立場(賛成か反対か)を決めましょう。

Step 3 Outlining

Think about two reasons or two pieces of evidence based on the information you have found through online search and group discussion in order to support your opinion. They will be the supporting sentences in the body of the paragraph.

オンライン・サーチで見つけた情報やグループで話し合ったことをもとに、自分の主張をサポートする理由・根拠を2つ考えてみましょう。これらはパラグラフの本文で支持文になります。

Reason/evidence 1

Reason/evidence 2

_____

_____

_____

Step 4 Writing a topic sentence

Write your opinion as a topic sentence (TS) after consulting the examples below.　　以下の例を参考にして、あなたの主張を話題文として書いてみましょう。

＜Agreement/賛成＞

> [TS1] People should learn English as a lingua franca.
> [TS2] Young Japanese should be encouraged to go abroad.
> [TS3] People should be encouraged to use SNS to communicate across borders.
> [TS4] Japanese society should welcome foreigners as nursing-care workers in Japan.

＜Disagreement/反対＞

> [TS1] It is not necessary for everyone to learn English as a lingua franca.
> [TS2] Going abroad is not always beneficial for all young Japanese.
> [TS3] SNS are not always convenient and useful.
> [TS4] The idea that Japan should accept foreign nursing-care workers is not a realistic solution.

Write your topic sentence.

_____

> Note : Avoid using *I think* when you sate your opinion. The English expression *I think* is not equal to 思います in Japanese; it makes your claim subjective without any evidence. You should avoid *I believe* for the same reason described above.
>
> メモ：*I think* という表現は使わないようにします。英語の *I think* は必ずしも日本語の「思います」に相当するわけではありません。*I think* を使うと主張が根拠のない主観的なものになってしまいます。同様の理由で *I believe* の使用も避けます。

Step 5 Writing an introductory sentence

Readers may feel it is abrupt if a paragraph starts with a topic sentence without any background. Thus, adding an introductory sentence (IS) before the topic sentence should give them a clear direction. See the examples below.

パラグラフを話題文で始めると、読者に唐突な印象を与えます。そこで、話題文の前に導入文を加えると、パラグラフの方向性がはっきりします。以下の例文を参考にしてください。

[IS1] More and more people use English when they do not speak the same language.

[IS2] English is often chosen as a lingua franca when people speak different languages.

[IS3] Nowadays, a large number of people go abroad to pursue their career.

[IS4] In this era of globalization, a large number of people move across borders.

[IS5] In this era of globalization, more and more people use social networking services (SNS).

[IS6] Nowadays, a large number of people use social networking services (SNS) such as GREE, Facebook, Twitter, and LINE.

[IS7] Japanese society is aging with more elderly and fewer young people.

[IS8] Japan has a big problem: a low birthrate and an aging population.

Connecting sentences

Add one more sentence between the introductory sentence and the topic sentence to make them flow smoothly. Furthermore, you should clearly state that you will provide two reasons to support your opinion.

2つの文がうまくつながるように、導入文と話題文をつなぐ文を挿入してみましょう。さらに、主張を支持する2つの理由があることも明確に述べます。

In the following examples : _____introductory sentence_____ ;
linking phrase/connecting sentence; ~~topic sentence~~

▭ = connecting phrase

Example 1 【Agreement on Topic 1】

More and more people use English when they do not speak the same language. In other words, English is used as a common language. Given this, business people should learn English as a lingua franca for two reasons.

Example 2 【Disagreement on Topic 1】

English is often chosen as a lingua franca when people speak different languages. For this reason, learning English is helpful. However, it is not necessary to learn English only because it is a lingua franca for two reasons.

Example 3 【Agreement on Topic 2】

Nowadays, a large number of people go abroad to pursue their career. Reportedly, however, the number of Japanese going overseas has decreased. There are two reasons why young Japanese should be encouraged to go abroad.

Example 4 【Disagreement on Topic 2】

In this era of globalization, a large number of people move across borders. Accordingly / As a result, young Japanese are often told to go abroad and see the world. However, it is not always beneficial for all young people to go abroad for two reasons.

Example 5 【Agreement on Topic 3】

In this era of globalization, more and more people use social networking services (SNS). Through this technology, they can communicate anytime and anywhere without meeting others face-to-face. People should be encouraged to use SNS for borderless communication for two reasons.

Example 6 【Disagreement on Topic 3】

Nowadays, a large number of people use social networking services (SNS) such as GREE, Facebook, Twitter, and LINE. With SNS, we can communicate with people around the world in an easy and quick way. However, there are two reasons why SNS are not always convenient and useful.

Example 7 【Agreement on Topic 4】

Japanese society is aging with more elderly and fewer young people. Considering this fact, it is predictable that there will be a shortage of Japanese staff in nursing homes. Given this, Japanese society should welcome foreigners as nursing-care workers for two reasons.

Example 8 【Disagreement on Topic 4】

Japan has a big problem : a low birthrate and an aging population. As a possible solution, the government has decided to accept foreigners to work as nursing-care workers in Japan. However, accepting foreign nursing-care workers is not realistic for two reasons.

Write your introductory and topic sentences with a connecting sentence as well as a linking phrase.

___

___

___

Step 6 Writing the body

Write two reasons or pieces of evidence to support your claim after consulting the examples below.

以下の例文を参考にして、主張を支持する理由、あるいは根拠を2つ書いてみましょう。

[Reason/evidence (1) as a main point & supporting sentences]
メイン・ポイントとしての理由・根拠（1）と支持文

In the following examples, ▇▇▇ indicates a connecting word or phrase.

＜Agreement/賛成＞

> [SS1-1] The primary reason for learning English is that it will bring you more business chances. In this era of globalization, many Japanese companies are moving overseas to expand their business. As a result, they require more people who can speak English.
>
> [SS1-2] First of all, people with overseas experience have an advantage working for a multi-national company. Exposure to different cultures abroad helps them expand their views. Consequently, it is easier for them to work with foreign employees.
>
> [SS1-3] The main support for this idea is that SNS can reconnect people who have lost touch with each other no matter where they are. Through SNS, you can find your old friends and people you met overseas. In this way, SNS can be a convenient tool to find someone with whom you want to stay in contact.
>
> [SS1-4] The first reason is that the employment of foreign nursing-care workers is one solution for the shortage of Japanese workers. In short, there is no reason to limit these jobs to Japanese only; foreigners should be allowed to work as long as they give good care for the elderly.

＜Disagreement/反対＞

[SS1-1] The primary reason against the idea is that not everyone has a chance to communicate in English. When you are at an international meeting, English is helpful as a common language for communicating with other participants. However, this does not happen for the majority of people in Japan.

[SS1-2] The primary reason is that overseas experience is not always advantageous in a job search. In particular, studying abroad is problematic when applying for jobs in Japan. By the time students come back to Japan, most companies have finished employment examinations for the following year.

[SS1-3] First of all, through SNS, personal information will be available for anyone to access. Therefore, you might receive some nasty messages and even be threatened. For this reason, SNS will increase the risk of being involved in a crime.

[SS1-4] The first serious concern over the issue is language problems. Admittedly, foreign workers have to know enough Japanese to pass the national examination for licensed nursing-care workers. However, the elderly do not always speak standard Japanese. This will make communication with them difficult for foreign workers.

Write your first main point and supporting sentences.

_____
_____
_____
_____

[Reason/evidence (2) as a main point & supporting sentences]

メイン・ポイントとしての理由・根拠 (2) と支持文

＜Agreement/賛成＞

[SS2-1] The second reason is that English will expand the number of resources available for businesses. Nowadays, more references, including books and Internet sites, some of which may not be available in the native language, are available in English than ever before. Therefore, people who can use English can get more information faster than those who cannot.

[SS2-2] The next reason is that overseas experience can make people more ambitious. Overcoming various difficulties abroad should help them develop a willingness to take on challenges. As a result, mental strength should be another advantage for them.

[SS2-3] Another main support is that SNS can easily connect people around the world. It gives them chances to encounter strangers who live on the other side of the earth online, regardless of where they live. In other words, SNS will be a useful tool to increase networking.

[SS2-4] The second reason is that the current situation in nursing care will encourage foreigners to come and work in Japan since Japanese consider nursing care a hard, dirty, and dangerous job. Consequently, few people are willing to work in nursing or retirement homes. This demands allowing foreign nursing-care workers.

＜Disagreement/反対＞

[SS2-1] The second reason is that not everyone will be successful in learning English. One individual difference is motivation : in particular, people may not be motivated when they do not have a clear purpose for learning a foreign language. For this reason, it is not efficient to force everyone to learn English.

[SS2-2] Another reason is that people with overseas experience will be isolated in society due to their culturally unacceptable behavior. When they come back, they often bring the behavior and values that they have adopted abroad into Japanese society. Therefore, their inappropriate manners will make them feel like outsiders.

[SS2-3] Next, SNS can be addictive : some people cannot stop being constantly connected online. As a result, they may feel left out when they are offline. Even worse, they can be the targets of bullying if they do not respond to messages immediately.

[SS2-4] Another serious concern is that Japan is not fully ready to accept people with different cultural backgrounds. In particular, Muslim people have had a hard time since Japanese are not familiar with their religious discipline. Therefore, the employment of foreign nursing-care workers will not be successful unless Japanese are educated in their cultural differences.

Write your second main point and supporting sentences.

_____

_____

_____

_____

Step 7 Writing a concluding sentence

Write a concluding sentence (CS). Remember that you must rephrase the topic sentence and should not add any new ideas. See the linking phrase box and example sentences below for reference. Two example CSs are provided for each topic.

結論文を書いてみましょう。結論文は話題文を言い換えるだけで、新しいことは書きません。以下のつなぎの語句と例を参考にしてください。ひとつのトピックに2つの結論文の例が提示されています。

Linking Phrase Box

> To sum up,
> In conclusion,
> As argued above,
> As stated above,
> As explained above,

[Example CSs]
＜Agreement/賛成＞

> [CS1] To sum up, learning English as a lingua franca benefits people with different language backgrounds.
> [CS2] As argued above, business people should learn English as a lingua franca in order to communicate with those who speak different languages.
>
> [CS3] In conclusion, young Japanese should go abroad for their own benefit.
> [CS4] As stated above, going abroad has benefits for young Japanese in terms of mental flexibility and strength.
>
> [CS5] To sum up, SNS are a remarkable tool for people to communicate across borders.
> [CS6] As explained above, SNS are beneficial for borderless communication.
>
> [CS7] In conclusion, accepting foreigners as nursing-care workers should be advantageous for Japan.
> [CS8] As argued above, foreign nursing-care workers should be welcomed in Japanese society.

＜Disagreement/反対＞

[CS1] To sum up, learning English should not be required for everyone.
[CS2] As argued above, learning English is beneficial for only a limited number of people.

[CS3] In conclusion, not everyone can enjoy the benefits of going abroad.
[CS4] As stated above, going abroad is not always beneficial for young Japanese.

[CS5] To sum up, the opinion that SNS are convenient and useful is misguided.
[CS6] As explained above, we can become involved in some problems because of SNS.

[CS7] In conclusion, accepting foreign nursing-care workers is not a realistic solution.
[CS8] As argued above, we will face some problems if we increasingly employ foreigners as nursing-care workers.

Write your concluding sentence.

_____

_____

Step 8 Writing a title

Now, write a title for your paragraph. It should give a hint for readers to predict what the main point is in the paragraph.

では、ここまで書いた文章にタイトルをつけてみましょう。読む人が文章の内容を推測できるタイトルを考えます。

Your title _____

Step 9 Typing the paragraph

Type all the sentences you have written following paragraph format (see Appendix A).

パラグラフ・フォーマットに従って、ここまで書いた文をタイプしてみましょう。フォーマットについては、付録Aを参照してください。

Advanced

Add a final thought/comment to the concluding sentence in order to end the paragraph.

結論文の後に一言加えてパラグラフを終了してみましょう。

<Agreement/賛成>

[FS1] A common language can promote more frequent interaction, leading to mutual understanding, which is necessary for successful negotiations.
[FS2] The overseas experience helps them grow as global citizens.
[FS3] In this sense, we are no longer limited by our geographic location.
[FS4] It is reasonable to solve domestic problems with help from outsiders.

<Disagreement/反対>

[FS1] Since a limited number of people use English as a lingua franca, it should only be learned when it is necessary.
[FS2] It should not be pushed unless they have a clear goal to achieve through overseas experience.
[FS3] It is dangerous to put too much trust in SNS.
[FS4] They should not be accepted unless the Japanese government is ready to provide necessary support programs for them.

Write your final sentence.

_____
_____
_____
_____

Chapter 12
Revision
Stating Your Opinion

We are at the revising stage. You will rewrite your first draft to make it more comprehensible.

修正の段階です。より分かりやすい文章になるようにファースト・ドラフトを書き換えてみます。

Step 1　Self-revision

Check your first draft with the checklist (see Appendix B).

付録Bのチェックリストを使って、ファースト・ドラフトを確認してください。

Step 2　Peer review

[Preparation]
(1) Type your individual sentences with extra space between the sentences.
(2) Cut them into strips. Each strip should have a single sentence.

（1）文と文の行間を十分にあけ、文をひとつずつタイプします。
（2）文ごとに切り離します。ひとつの紙片にひとつの文とします。

Exchange your strips with a classmate. Put your partner's sentences in order. Leave aside any ones you think do not fit in the paragraph.

クラスメートと紙片の束を交換します。パートナーの紙片を順番に並べてみてください。パラグラフのどこにも当てはまらないと思う文は横へ出しておきます。

Check your partner's order for your sentences.

並べてもらった紙片を確認してみましょう。

Step 3　Reorganizing the body : rewriting your main points and supporting sentences

Considering your partner's order for your sentences, rewrite your first draft. During revision, you should rethink the order of your sentences, add and/or delete some sentences, and/or rephrase sentences. Also, ask your partner for his or her suggestions and comments.

先ほど並べてもらった順番を参考に、ファースト・ドラフトを書き直します。文の順番を変えたり、文を追加、あるいは削除したり、文を言い換えたりして修正していきます。また、パートナーに提案や意見を聞いてもよいでしょう。

Step 4　Rethinking and rewriting your topic sentence and concluding sentence

Rethink your topic and concluding sentences as well. Rewrite them if necessary.

話題文と結論文を再考してみましょう。必要であれば、書き直します。

【Revised topic sentence (書き直した話題文)】

_____

_____

【Revised concluding sentence (書き直した結論文)】

_____

_____

Step 5　Rethinking the title

Rethink the title. Is it clear and concrete enough for readers to guess the content of the paragraph? If not, you need to rewrite it.

タイトルを再考してみましょう。読者がパラグラフの内容を予測するために明確で具体的なタイトルになっていますか。そうでないと思ったら書き直しましょう。

【Revised title (書き直したタイトル)】

_____

Before the next class

Check your second draft with the checklist (see Appendix C) before you bring it to the next class.

次の授業にセカンド・ドラフトを持って行く前に、付録Cのチェックリストを使って、セカンド・ドラフトを確認してみましょう。

Peer review in class

Read and check a classmate's second draft, referring to the peer review sheet (see Appendix D).

クラスメートが書いたセカンド・ドラフトを、付録Dのピア・レビュー・シートに従って確認してみましょう。

Then, exchange comments on each other's paragraphs.

その後、お互いのパラグラフについてコメントをしてみましょう。

Sentence Exercise (1)   Connecting sentences

You will find a gap marked by △ between two sentences. Provide an appropriate conjunction to connect them smoothly, choosing from these suggested conjunctions : *although, and, because, for example, however, in other words, on the contrary, so, therefore, when*. You may need to change the order of sentences.

1. I am shy. △ I do not like to talk to anyone whom I do not know well.

2. I get tense. △ I stand up and talk in front of other people.

3. I am an honest person. △ I do not like to lie. △ I tell my opinion straight.

4. People think that I am optimistic. △ I am a nervous person. △ I worry about little things.

5. I am a shy person. △ I am nervous with strangers. △ It was very hard for me to talk to friends' mothers when I was a child.

Sentence Exercise (2) Meaningful relationship between subject and verb

Read the following sentences and decide whether they make sense to you. What makes them strange in terms of meaning? Then, rewrite them into meaningful sentences.

1. Today died my dog in Fukuoka.

2. The sea lives many jellyfish.

3. Today blew strong wind.

4. The test did well than I expected.

5. Monday morning feels so tired.

6. Okinawa was issued a typhoon warning.

7. All dishes are used tomatoes at this restaurant.

Sentence Exercise (3) — Long sentences

The following sentences are too long to clearly understand the writer's intended meaning. What message do you think he or she is trying to express to readers? How would you rewrite the sentences to convey the writer's intended meaning? You may need to change the order of phrases or add words and phrases to make it clear.

1. Although I still like storybooks, because I am interested in how people live their lives, I tend to read famous people's biographies when I am worried about my future.

2. Before I came to Okinawa, I was excited about my new life living by myself, although I found that it was more difficult than I thought.

3. When I started the first term in the first year at the university, I often skipped classes because I got homesick unexpectedly, even though I looked forward to living by myself and meeting new people at school.

Appendix A (付録A) — Paragraph format rules

There are format rules you need to follow for formal paragraph writing.

パラグラフのフォーマットに関して以下の決まりがあります。

1. Write your name, student identification number, and the date in the top right-hand corner. This section is called the heading.

2. Write the title in the center of the first line.

3. In titles, capitalize the first letter of the first word, the last word, and all major words, including nouns, verbs, adjectives, adverbs, and pronouns. On the other hand, function words including articles (e.g., *a*, *an*, *the*), short prepositions (e.g., *to*, *with*, *at*), and conjunctions (e.g., *and*, *but*) should not be capitalized. Note that the first letter of the last word and all words of more than four letters must always be capitalized even if they are function words, such as *When John Walked In*.

4. Skip a line between the title and the paragraph.

5. Indent at the beginning of a paragraph, using the tab key on the computer.

6. Leave 2.5 cm margins.

7. Use a period, exclamation mark, or question mark at the end of every sentence.

8. Leave 1 space after periods.

9. Begin every sentence with a capital letter.

10. Capitalize names of people and places as well.

11. Periods and commas must follow words. They can't begin a new line or come after a space.

12. Every sentence in a paragraph follows the sentence before it. Start on a new line only when you begin a new paragraph.

1. 右上端に氏名、学籍番号、提出日を書く。この部分をヘディングと呼ぶ。
2. タイトルを真ん中に書く。
3. タイトルでは、最初と最後の単語および名詞、動詞、形容詞、副詞、代名詞は最初の文字を大文字にする。一方、機能語（冠詞、4文字より短い前置詞、接続詞など）の最初の文字は小文字でよい。ただし、最後の単語や4文字以上の語は、たとえ機能語であっても最初の文字は大文字にする（例えば、When John Walked In）。
4. タイトルと段落の間は一行あける。
5. コンピュータのタブキーを使って、段落の始めはインデントする。

6. 余白は上下左右2.5センチ取る。
7. 各文の最後は、ピリオド、感嘆符、疑問符をつける。
8. ピリオドと次の文との間にスペースをひとつあける。
9. 文は常に大文字で書き始める。
10. 人名、場所の名前の最初は大文字にする。
11. ピリオドやコンマは必ず語に続ける。改行して行の最初にピリオドやコンマをつけない。
12. 次の文は必ず前の文に続けて書く。新しい段落を始める場合以外は改行しない。

Exercise

Format the following paragraph by using the format rules above.

フォーマットの規則に従って、次のパラグラフを書き直してみましょう。

---

my classmate from Hiroshima
Daisuke Hayashi is one of my classmates in my english class. He is from Hiroshima and lives in Okinawa now
he likes marine sports Especially scuba diving. That is why he decided to move to a semi-tropical island, Okinawa.
He wakes up at 5:00 almost every weekend and goes scuba diving. He has many friends whom he has met through scuba diving. Some of them are from abroad so he often speaks English with them. I think his English is very good
.
Daisuke loves Okinawa since people are very kind and it is warm in the winter. He also likes Okinawan art and music. He is planning to stay here after he graduates from the university.

Compare your answers with the answer key below.

以下の解答と比べてみましょう。

[Answer key]

Akira Ishikawa
1234567
April 17, 2014

My Classmate from Hiroshima

   Daisuke Hayashi is one of my classmates in my English class. He is from Hiroshima and lives in Okinawa now. He likes marine sports, especially scuba diving. That is why he decided to move to a semi-tropical island, Okinawa. He wakes up at 5:00 almost every weekend and goes scuba diving. He has many friends whom he has met through scuba diving. Some of them are from abroad, so he often speaks English with them. I think his English is very good.

    Daisuke loves Okinawa since people are very kind, and it is warm in the winter. He also likes Okinawan art and music. He is planning to stay here after he graduates from the university.

Appendix B (付録B) ファースト・ドラフト チェックリスト

1. このパラグラフで読者に一番伝えたいことは何ですか。具体的な説明を書いてみましょう。

_____

_____

_____

_____

_____

2. それぞれの項目を確認しましょう。✓がつかない項目は修正して、ドラフトを書き直します。

チェック項目	確認・済み
1. パラグラフの内容が予想できるタイトルですか。	
2. 話題文はありますか。話題文に下線を引いてみましょう。	
3. 話題文にメイン・アイデアがはっきりと書かれていますか。	
4. メイン・ポイントは話題文を説明する内容ですか。	
5. それぞれのメイン・ポイントを説明する支持文が書かれていますか。	
6. 結論文はありますか。結論文に二重下線を引いてください。	
7. 結論文は話題文と同じ内容ですか。	
8. つなぎの語句を使うなどして、前の文から次の文へはスムーズにつながっていますか。	

Appendix C (付録C)　セカンド・ドラフト　チェックリスト

1. それぞれの項目を確認しましょう。✓がつかない項目は修正して、ドラフトを書き直します。

チェック項目	確認・済み
1. タイトルの書き方は適切ですか。	
2. 段落の最初の文は、インデントされていますか。	
3. カンマで文がつながれていませんか。 　　例：×I am shy, I am not good at talking to strangers.	
4. Becauseの節には主節がありますか。 　　例：×Because I like music.	
5. And, But, Soなどの接続詞で文が始まっていませんか。	
6. 接続詞の後にカンマがついたりしていませんか。 　　例：×but, ; ×and,; ×because,	
7. 短文や単文の羅列になっていませんか。 　　➡ できるだけ従属接続詞あるいは同格接続詞を使ってつなげましょう。	
8. 省略形を使っていませんか。 　　例 ×I'm → ○I am; ×can't → ○cannot; ×haven't → ○have not; ×don't → ○do not	

2. 内容について

1. a. 話題文に下線を引いてください。 　　b. より分かりやすい話題文にするために、どのような工夫をしましたか。
2. 支持文とその説明文にはどのような工夫をしましたか。
3. a. 結論文に下線を引いてください。 　　b. より分かりやすい結論文にするために、どのような工夫をしましたか。

Appendix D (付録D) ピア・レビュー・シート

ドラフトをチェックした人：　　　　　　　　ドラフトを書いた人：

＊質問に当てはまるものにひとつだけ○をつける。

1. タイトルからパラグラフの内容が予想できますか。　　　　　　［できる・あまりできない］＊

2. 話題文に下線を引いてください。

3. 話題文を読んで、書き手が一番伝えたいことは何だと思いますか。

　_____

　_____

4. メイン・ポイントはいくつありますか。

5. メイン・ポイントの導入が分かる語句が使われていますか。［使われている・あまり使われていない］＊

6. それぞれのメイン・ポイントは書き手の主張をサポートしていますか。

　　　　　　　　　［している・どちらかと言えばしている・サポートしているとは言えない］＊

7. 支持文は分かりやすいですか。

　　　　　　　　　［分かりやすい・どちらかと言えば分かりやすい・分かりやすいとは言えない］＊

8. 説明不足だと思う箇所に△を挿入してください。

9. 結論文に二重下線を引いてください。

10. 結論文は話題文と同じ内容になっていますか。　　　　　　　　　　［はい・いいえ］＊

11. パラグラフの内容はタイトルから予想した通りでしたか。

　　　　　　　　　　　　　　　　　　　　　［はい・どちらかと言えば予想通り・いいえ］＊

12. よく分からない箇所に波線を引いてください。

13. クラスメートが書いたパラグラフのよい点は何ですか。

　_____

　_____

14. どのような工夫や修正をするとよりよいパラグラフになると思いますか。

　_____

JPCA

日本出版著作権協会
http://www.jpca.jp.net/

本書は日本出版著作権協会（JPCA）が委託管理する著作物です。
複写（コピー）・複製、その他著作物の利用については、事前に JPCA（電話 03-3812-9424、e-mail:info@e-jpca.com）の許諾を得て下さい。なお、無断でコピー・スキャン・デジタル化等の複製をすることは著作権法上の例外を除き、著作権法違反となります。

A Guide with Models for Process Writing
モデルで学ぶプロセス・ライティング入門

2015 年 4 月 10 日　初版第 1 刷発行
2022 年 4 月 5 日　初版第 4 刷発行

著　者　柴田美紀

発行者　森　信久
発行所　**株式会社　松 柏 社**
　　　　〒102-0072　東京都千代田区飯田橋 1-6-1
　　　　TEL　03 (3230) 4813（代表）
　　　　FAX　03 (3230) 4857
　　　　http://www.shohakusha.com
　　　　e-mail: info@shohakusha.com

装　幀　　　　　小島トシノブ（NONdesign）
装画・挿絵　　　永野敬子
本文組版レイアウト　有限会社ケークルーデザインワークス
　　　　　　　　福田麻喜子／藤井　洋／大谷直也／神宮理恵
印　刷　　　　　中央精版印刷株式会社
ISBN978-4-88198-709-4
略号＝ 709
Copyright © 2015 by Miki Shibata

本書を無断で複写・複製することを禁じます。
落丁・乱丁は送料小社負担にてお取り替え致します。